THE SECRET LIFE OF
CORALS

Sex, War, and Rocks
That Don't Roll

David E. Vaughan, PhD

J.ROSS
PUBLISHING

ISBN: 978-1-60427-188-1

e-ISBN: 978-1-60427-836-1

Printed and bound in the U.S.A. Printed on acid-free paper.

10 9 8 7 6 5 4 3 2 1

Cover design by Kavita Razzaq

Library of Congress Cataloging-in-Publication Data
Names: Vaughan, David E., author.
Title: The secret life of corals : sex, war, and rocks that don't roll / by
    David Vaughan.
Description: Plantation, FL : J. Ross Publishing, [2023] | Includes
    bibliographical references and index. |
Identifiers: LCCN 2022027771 (print) | LCCN 2022027772
    (ebook) | ISBN 9781604271881 (hardcover) | ISBN
    9781604278361 (epub)
Subjects: LCSH: Corals. | Corals--Habitat. | Coral reef ecology. |
    BISAC: NATURE / Animals / Marine Life | NATURE / Envi-
    ronmental Conservation & Protection
Classification: LCC QL377.C5 V28 2023 (print) | LCC QL377.C5
    (ebook) | DDC 593.6--dc23/eng/20220614
LC record available at https://lccn.loc.gov/2022027771
LC ebook record available at https://lccn.loc.gov/2022027772

Direct all inquiries to J. Ross Publishing, Inc., 151 N. Nob Hill Rd., #476, Plantation, FL 33324.

Web: www.jrosspub.com

Table of Contents

Preface

*"Through the window of my mask I see a wall of coral,
its surface a living kaleidoscope of lilac flecks, splashes of gold,
reddish streaks and yellows, all tinged by the transparent blue of the sea."*
—Jacques Yves Cousteau

Corals are the gems of the oceans, creating the beautiful colors and shapes that form our reefs. Their story, told in the following pages, is unlike any story in the animal or plant kingdoms.

Once you learn about the secret life of corals, you will understand that they serve many vital functions for life on this planet. They create habitat for a large percentage of the seafood eaten around the world. As guardians of our coastlines, they absorb the brunt force of waves and tidal surges, particularly during tropical storms and hurricanes. When we breathe, we can thank corals because they contribute oxygen to the atmosphere. Corals also add significantly to our economy through tourism dollars and related jobs and industries. While they live under the sea, corals are truly important to our lives on land.

Although they are very beneficial to *our* existence, corals are quite precious in their own right. The individual coral polyps are nothing if not charming. The colonies they build and live in can be exquisite, with an amazing array of colors and shapes. These colonies can be large or small, branching, round, mountainous, plate-shaped, and more. Coral reefs can stretch for miles and team with fish and many other creatures such as crabs, shrimp, starfish, eels, rays, and lobsters.

The way corals behave is remarkable too. How they grow, reproduce, coordinate with one another, and even go to war is absolutely fascinating.

Unfortunately, since the 1950s, we have lost over half our coral reefs worldwide, primarily due to climate change and disease. Environmental stressors are devastating coral communities; however, there are corals that do persist. Somehow, they survive warming ocean temperatures, increasing ocean acidity, and various coral diseases. These are the corals we need to grow and replant back onto the reefs. The good news is that we can do it. We now have the technology, including methods to produce corals at scale by the hundreds of thousands—much faster than anyone ever thought possible.

Over the past 50 years I have worked at some of the most prestigious marine research institutions in the world and produced over 50 scientific publications. In 2021 I edited *Active Coral Restoration: Techniques for a Changing Planet*, the first comprehensive book on the subject, geared for the scientific community. Soon after, I realized that the story about corals, what they are exactly, why they are important, what is happening to them, and what we can do to restore them, needed to be conveyed to the rest of the world. For this reason, I was compelled to write this book.

My hope is that you will first fall in love with the crazy creature we call coral, and develop a genuine appreciation for this unique life form. In addition, I hope you will learn why they are so important to the marine environment and to our lives, what threats they are now facing, and how we can work together to "turn the tide" for corals.

—David Vaughan

Introduction: Dave's Journey

Submerged from the Start

When I was young, I didn't know my life's work would be corals, but I did know I wanted to spend it underwater. My fascination with the ocean world started at age 11 when I became obsessed with the thought of becoming a scuba diver like Jacques Yves Cousteau. While other children my age were writing book reports on fighter pilots, football players, and cowboys, I was deeply immersed in the writings of Cousteau and his colleague Frederick Dumas. Both men were instrumental in developing tools and equipment used for exploring the ocean. They are much better known, though, for bringing the undersea world into the homes of millions through television documentaries, movies, and books.

Imagine my disappointment when I discovered that scuba diving was an adult sport, with no serious equipment available for children. Not easily discouraged, I started to teach myself to hold my breath for long periods of time. My teachers undoubtedly thought me odd when they saw me hold my breath at my desk, turn red, and then exhale—as if clearing my imaginary snorkel.

In the summers I practiced holding my breath in our backyard swimming pool until I could hold it for 1–2 minutes—worrying the adults watching and waiting for me to resurface. At my family's summer home along the Jersey Shore, I spent my days underwater at the beach, searching for crustaceans, fish, clams, and seaweed while everyone else was riding the waves. Little did I realize that the trajectory of my life was already set in motion and that I would eventually become a marine biologist and grow many of these same organisms over the span of the next 50 years.

My parents hoped my obsession with scuba diving was just a passing phase. That began to change when my father came down the basement stairs and caught me melting down lead figures of toy soldiers, cowboys, and Indians. Once these favorite childhood toys were melted, I poured the liquid lead into a homemade mold to create my own custom dive weights. These would be used for the weight belt I hoped to proudly wear scuba diving. It was then that he and my mother realized I was not going to give up until someone of a higher authority explained why I was not ready for scuba diving.

So, my Dad took me to the few nearby dive centers. At each one, they confirmed I was indeed too young to learn to scuba dive. Plus, I was much too small to pick up a tank, let alone carry one on my back. I convinced my parents to take me to just one last shop an hour's drive away. It was a new business facility that belonged to a company that primarily built in-ground swimming pools. They also taught scuba diving in a small, deep showroom pool that had a window on the side for observation. At the time I was barely 3½ feet tall and 48 pounds at most. To me, the shop's 6-foot instructor who must have weighed two hundred pounds seemed a giant. My father asked him to teach me a few basic dive skills, hoping he too would agree I was much too young.

When I quickly connected the steel scuba tank to the backpack, attached the regulator, put on the tank that weighed almost as much as I did and jumped into the pool, the instructor gasped. He grabbed his tank like it was a toy and followed me in.

He gave me a workout typically reserved for the final underwater exam. He turned off my air, pulled off my mask and spun me around. My previous practice of holding my breath paid off. I easily waited, casually turned my air back on, cleared my regulator, and replaced my mask. Each time he spun me around, my head came back to the viewing window and I could see the terror in my parents' faces as they thought I might drown. But no, I was having the time of my life! To the instructor's amazement, I then said to him, "Is that all you got?" I'd passed the test. From then on my parents dutifully drove me to scuba lessons each week. In the end they were very proud when I received my scuba certification just prior to my thirteenth birthday.

Soon afterward, I had the opportunity to go on a science expedition to collect and study corals in the U.S. Virgin Islands, an amazing trip for a 13-year-old. My father made it possible and I am forever grateful. As the development officer for Fairleigh Dickenson University, he was responsible for raising funds. Professors from the college approached him about raising a million dollars to search for and develop a new marine laboratory in the Caribbean. (Years later, this endeavor resulted in the West Indies Marine Laboratory, eventually located on Saint Croix.)

My father agreed to try to raise the funds, first for the expedition, and then ultimately for laboratory construction. However, he threw in one condition: they take me along on the expedition. The professors agreed and probably thought I would hang out with the kids of the other professors, enjoying the pool and hotel amenities. But nope, I stayed in a tent on the beach with the college students who hoped they would not have to babysit me.

To my surprise, I was told to pack a geological chisel, hammer, or a prospector's tool for the expedition. Yep, my job was to break off live pieces of coral, and then dry them out in the sun, where they would unfortunately die. These coral samples were then sent back to the university laboratory where they were put in formalin jars and archived. Times have changed and this would not be done today unless you were taking small tissue samples for cloning corals for future restoration.

Each day's activities were memorable and mostly consisted of snorkeling from shore to gather various species of coral for the collection. Wading through the water I searched for an area without coral where I could comfortably sit and put on my fins. This took a while because there were so many staghorn and finger corals, a rare sight today. I vividly remember thinking, "I can hardly wait to get past all of these corals into deeper water to find more interesting corals like brain coral." The reef then was healthy and teeming with life. Sea urchins were everywhere. Sitting or standing on the reef was out of the question lest you impale yourself on one of these long-spined creatures. Naively, I thought that these healthy reefs would be around forever.

The expedition to the Virgin Islands was absolutely life changing for me. As time moved on my interests expanded to all forms of aquatic life, from marine plants and animals to wetland habitats. I saw beauty and intelligence in all creation. College was the next step and I attended a mid-western church college now called Graceland University. Although it may seem strange for an aspiring marine biologist to attend school in Iowa, this school encouraged my reverence for the natural world.

Later, I earned my Master's degree in biology at Fairleigh Dickinson University and worked with both marine algae and shellfish. My interest in micro algae and phytoplankton continued as they were in great demand specifically by shellfish hatcheries near the Jersey Shore. Many shellfish hatcheries were run by zoologists or malacologists that have studied clams or oysters, but did not know how to grow marine plants. And if you can't raise the right type of algae to feed bivalve larvae, they will ultimately starve and die. I knew very little about other marine invertebrates, but I could grow the heck out of algae.

I continued my education as a PhD candidate at Rutgers University. I was in the Botany and Plant Physiology Department and studied seagrasses and the microscopic algae that live on the surface of their leaves. My research led me to the Rutgers Marine Field Station in Tuckerton, New Jersey, to carry out fieldwork. In Tuckerton there was an old U.S. Coast Guard station, complete with a light tower at the tip of a ten-mile-long marsh peninsula. This station was given to the University because it was so remote that the Coast Guard had trouble keeping it manned. Apparently, the university did too, so I was offered the position of "graduate resident" and had the honor of living in the lighthouse-style structure while completing my field work for the next 4 and a half years.

During this time period, my brother, sister, and I had also been running a summer business venture to help finance our respective years in graduate school. We bought and operated an existing farmer's market that sold vegetables, plants, and local seafood. In the first year we had trouble getting the supply of plants needed to fill our orders. Immediately, I was catapulted into plant production and built our first greenhouse. Every year we built a new greenhouse and eventually had an entire greenhouse production system so we could grow and sell thousands (instead of hundreds) of geraniums, marigolds, and petunias.

My life was plants, plants, and more plants, until finally clams became my focus. At our farmers market, we also sold local harvested clams, but one year we could not keep them stocked due to high demand. It did not take long for me to realize, "Hey, when we needed greenhouse plants we grew them, now we need clams. I am a marine biologist, there must be something I can do." I started to thoroughly research how to grow clams. My wife, Donna, would use the term "ad nauseam." One time she came downstairs in the middle of the night to find me and one of my fellow grad students, Joe, staring at a small glass aquarium tank containing just one male and one female chowder size clam and proclaiming we were going to witness them spawn. After a while she gave up and went to sleep. Early the next morning, she found Joe and me still awake staring into a milky white tank now full of clam sperm and eggs. They had done it! I think she knew then and there that our future would change, and she was right—although my in-depth work with clams would come a few years later. My siblings and I kept growing greenhouse plants and selling them at the farmers market over the next several years while also finishing our respective degrees.

Once I had my PhD, my sister and I left the business in the capable hands of our brother who still owns and operates it in New Jersey to this day. If you are ever near Ocean City, stop by Vaughan's Farm & Market and say hi to John. My sister, Pam, went on to become a professor at Stockton University and I followed my interest in clams. First, I formed Aqua-Farms, a commercial clam hatchery, then moved on to Cultured Aquatics on Long Island, and finally went off to Florida to scale up shellfish culture.

For the next 20 years, my work with clams and oysters occurred at Harbor Branch Oceanographic Institute in Florida as Director of the Aquaculture Division. During this time we scaled up clam culture technology by improving the hatchery—spawning tanks where clam larvae, also known as seed, are formed. We went from producing 1 million clam seed per year to producing 1 million clam seed per day, and eventually reached a total of a billion produced before I left. During that time I was given the nickname "Dr. Clam." This production of selected clam seed was so successful that we were able to open "Clam College" which provided education and training in clam farming to displaced fishermen.

We were able to grow out our business to support other research programs, such as the development of culture technologies for the production of marine ornamentals (fish, plants, invertebrates, corals) for the aquarium trade. The impetus for this was to farm these plants and animals in tanks instead of being harvested or taken from the reef. We started our research with clown fish, also known as the anemone fish, a year before the Disney movie "Finding Nemo" came out.

By then we had developed the technology to produce 25,000 fish per month and with demand soaring turned the research hatchery into a for-profit company called Oceans, Reefs and Aquariums, Inc. (ORA).

From this revenue we decided to culture corals for the aquarium trade. At that time, all corals from the Atlantic and Caribbean were protected, so only corals from the Pacific Ocean were legal to buy. It was not long before we scaled up to 100,000 corals cultured for the aquarium trade. We continued to grow and sell these corals with hopes that the process of importing wild coral from the Pacific Ocean would slow down or stop altogether.

It was around this time I had the pleasure of meeting Alexandra and Philippe Cousteau, the grandchildren of my childhood hero Jacques Cousteau. They wanted to tour the aquaculture facilities at Harbor Branch, and I was more than happy to show them around. After the tour they asked why were we growing corals for the aquarium trade? I replied, "To decrease the number of corals taken off reefs in the wild." Philippe then asked, "Why are you not growing these corals *for* the reefs, growing them and putting them back out to sea?"

In that instant my life changed again. Philippe, Alexandra, and I started the "International Coral Restoration Initiative," and a new adventure began. I left Harbor Branch, purchased a warehouse nearby, and started growing corals for outplanting. We continued for three years, but sadly, all our hard work was lost when two consecutive hurricanes, Frances and Jean, struck South Florida in 2004. The area was devastated. Our project came to a halt, and my house was destroyed. In the aftermath, Philippe and Alexandra left for Washington, D.C., and I took a new position at Mote Marine Laboratory in the Florida Keys.

During the next 15 years at Mote Marine Laboratory as the Executive Director of the Tropical Research Lab (now the International Center for Coral Reef Research and

Restoration), I continued my passion for trying to grow corals at scale—hoping to then plant them back onto the reefs for restoration. We focused on coral species found in the waters off the coast of Florida and in the Caribbean, particularly the reef-building coral species which are more massive in size.

At this time people were fragmenting/breaking the one branching coral, known as staghorn coral, and growing them in the field for restoration purposes. To my amazement though, nobody was trying to grow the other 26 species of massive corals, which I termed *orphan corals*. When I asked about hatching (breeding) these corals in a nursery, in addition to breaking and growing them, I was told no one did that. So we decided to try. We worked through a normal marine hatchery process similar to what I used with clams, oysters, and fish. To our amazement we were able to produce a dozen of the first "test-tube baby corals" from elkhorn coral gametes collected in the wild. Although hatching the coral in the lab was successful, the coral larvae grew very, very slowly. At three months they were still too small to see with the naked eye. By six months they were barely visible, and after 1-3 years of age they were still only about the size of a coin.

Frustrated, I realized the growth rate was just too slow to grow these corals at scale in a timely fashion. So, I moved these corals from their perch on the top shelf of a PVC frame to the bottom of the tank. For the better part of a year, I forgot about them.

One day I went to move them so that I could clean the tank. One of the corals was stuck to the bottom. I yanked and yanked until I heard a crack! It broke into a dozen tiny pieces. I thought for sure that I had killed it or at best caused a huge setback in its attempt to grow. But I was wrong! What happened next is what the *New York Times* called "My Eureka Mistake." It turned out to be a game-changer for corals and will be discussed further in Chapter 18 (to keep you in suspense).

My life to date has been serendipitous, and sometimes it has seemed cosmically planned to get me to this point. Although I did not know it at the time, my work with algae, clams, oysters, and fish was essential in helping me to eventually develop technological systems for growing corals in very large numbers (at scale). My Eureka Mistake then paved the way for coral growth and restoration nobody ever thought possible, including myself. I now have a foundation called "Plant a Million Corals" and I am dedicated to growing and planting a million corals before I retire.

The pages of this book represent a lifetime of work and trial and error. My career as a marine biologist has given me an insight into corals that few can match. I am so excited for you to dive in with me and learn about the secret life of corals: what they actually are; their journey from larvae to solid members of the reef; how they eat, have sex, and go to war; their importance to the planet; how they are dealing with environmental stressors; and how new technologies for restoration are providing hope for their future. They are truly remarkable, a creature like no other. Let's learn about and protect them together!

This is the Johnson Sea Link Submersible, the vessel that took Dr. Vaughan on his deepest ocean journey (2,000+ feet) to research deep sea mollusks and corals that could be cultured for biomedical uses (see Chapter 13). Pictured is Dr. Vaughan (right) and family, Dee Dee and Jason.

PART I

What Is a Coral?

Manta ray approaching a coral reef in the Maldives, Indian Ocean.

1

The Importance of Coral Reefs

DESPITE BEING mostly water, when it came time to name our planet, land-loving humans thought *Planet Earth* would be best, going so far as to make the word "earth" synonymous with the very soil we cultivate and walk upon. When viewed from space, however, we get an entirely different picture, one where the name *Blue Planet* makes a lot more sense. Oceans cover 71% of the earth's surface—they are the dominant and defining body of our home.

Throughout history, people have roamed, explored, and expanded civilization on Earth into uncharted territories. Historically, ocean-based travel by boat or ship was essentially for commerce and the relocation of people. The world of the seas was known only from the surface and by what was caught and brought aboard for food. Most early seafarers saw the ocean as a mysterious place with sea monsters ready to drag down a ship to its watery grave, perhaps with a mermaid to sing them a siren's song along the way. With occasional glimpses of sharks, whales, rays, enormous jelly fish, and other animals, their imaginations could easily create tales of terror due to their lack of understanding. Coral reefs were dangerous areas close to the surface that could strand or destroy ships and were to be avoided at all costs. The amazing color, variety of life, and unique beauty that abounds below the surface was hidden from their view.

We now know that coral reefs are some of the most diverse and valuable ecosystems on this *Blue Planet* of ours. Healthy reefs are full of unique life-forms, and they can be quite expansive. Coral reefs are actually living rock-like structures. They are made up of distinct coral colonies that are different shapes and colors depending on the species of coral. These coral colonies are made up of individual coral polyps. Their fascinating biology and life history will be explored in future chapters. For now, we will focus on the coral reef as a whole.

A majority of corals that build coral reefs are found in warm tropical waters close to the equator. Different species of corals live in different ocean basins, so reefs in the Indo-Pacific Ocean region can look different from reefs in the tropical western Atlantic Ocean. The Indo-Pacific Ocean region extends from the Red Sea and the Persian Gulf through the Indian and Pacific Oceans to the western coast of Panama. Western Atlantic reefs are found in the waters of Bermuda, the Bahamas, the Caribbean Islands, Belize, Florida, and the Gulf of Mexico.[1] Corals also grow on rocky outcrops in some areas of the Gulf of California. Healthy coral reefs in all these areas can be absolutely striking in color and shape, providing habitat for an enormous amount of marine life.

Although people appreciate that coral reefs are spectacular to see, many are unaware as to how vital they actually are to life on this planet. In fact, throughout my career I have often been asked, "Just how important are coral reefs, anyway?" The answer is more complex than one might think and takes some time to fully explain. Corals and the reefs they create offer so many valuable services to both the marine environment and our own lives that they are among the key drivers of human health, nutrition, safety, economic well-being, and survival on the planet. Coral reefs provide habitat for a large portion of the seafood that we consume. In addition, they provide subsistence living in terms of daily food for almost a billion people worldwide. They protect our coastlines during storm events (i.e., hurricanes) and they even add oxygen to the air that we breathe. They are a major contributor to our economy through tourism and the jobs that support it. And lastly, coral reefs are considered key to finding new medicines for the 21st century. Those who asked the initial question are usually surprised by this answer so we will go into more detail in the following sections.

Corals Produce Oxygen

It is a little-known fact that the majority of oxygen we breathe on land is produced in the ocean. It was originally thought that the vast number of trees and plants in the forest were the major suppliers of oxygen, but that is not the case. We hear that the rain forests are the "lungs of our planet" and they are certainly one of the heavy lifters in the production of oxygen. I would argue, however, that the true lungs of the earth rest beneath the surface of our oceans.

Most scientists believe between 50–80% of the oxygen we breathe comes from the oceans.[2] It is produced by marine plants of all sizes, from microscopic algae like phytoplankton, to giant kelp that can reach up to 65 meters in length. What is surprising is that all reef-building corals have algae that live inside of them, and they produce oxygen as well. This oxygen produced by marine plants is released into the water, which then travels to the ocean surface where it escapes into the atmosphere.

In many of my presentations I ask the audience to take a breath. They usually comply with a half-hearted inhale and exhale. Then I encourage them to take another—bigger and deeper—which usually gets the more energetic response I was looking for. This exercise is not to wake them up and get them to listen more attentively, but to demonstrate one of the biggest, most relatable values of corals to society. We breathe the oxygen that corals produce. I ask the audience to consider that second, deeper breath as a "breath of gratitude" for the oceans and the corals within them.

Habitat for Seafood

Many people do not typically correlate their enjoyment of seafood to corals, after all, no restaurant has coral on the menu. However, coral reefs, which occupy less than 1% of the ocean floor, support 25–40% of our commercial fisheries![3] This translates to food on our plates and dollars pumped into our economy. The National Marine Fisheries Service estimates the commercial value of U.S. fisheries from coral reefs is over 100 million dollars.[4] Around the world, indigenous people in tropical island nations subsist on local seafood caught in and around coral reefs. It is the coral reef that provides places for creatures large and small, solitary or schooling, to survive and flourish.

The huge area that covers the bottom of our oceans is mostly sand or mud bottom terrain, so a dynamic reef ecosystem is like an oasis in the middle of a desert. This unique, diverse, three-dimensional habitat provides structure with nooks and crannies for all types of marine life to thrive. This includes the finfish swimming over the reef, as well as the lobsters, crabs, mollusks, and other invertebrates hidden within it. Many seafood species use the reef as a permanent home, others use the reef to breed and raise their young, and some come to the reef just to feed.

Unfortunately, demand for fresh seafood is rising and ocean harvests are already becoming unsustainable for many of the species that are fished worldwide. In addition, we are losing critical coral reef habitat due to disease and effects from climate change. If you don't like eating seafood this may not seem like a problem, but the impact goes beyond just the unquenchable appetite for seafood shared by many around the world.

Tourism

Tourism is a large component of the economic engine that runs throughout the tropics as tourists like to fish, scuba dive, and snorkel on coral reefs. These reefs are the primary reason why people visit these locations. Many of these areas with local reefs may have thousands of residents and millions of visiting tourists throughout the year. Vacationers help the local economy by eating at restaurants, staying at hotels, and renting boats, kayaks, and dive equipment. They also pay for charter boats, complete with captain and crew, to take them diving and fishing. In South Florida alone, corals are responsible for over 70,000 jobs—estimated by the National Oceanic and Atmospheric Administration (NOAA) to be worth over five billion dollars (with a "B") per year.[5] These values are similar for Hawaii and the Great Barrier Reef in Australia. So, the health of coral reefs is definitively linked to the economy of coastal areas in tropical regions.

Shoreline Protection

Many people don't know that coral reefs provide an amazing amount of shoreline protection, but that is exactly what they do. Coastal wetlands protect seaside communities during hurricanes by breaking up the energy of the waves. Coral reefs behave the same way—they are the underwater defenses for damaging waves in tropical areas. The barrier reefs take the first big waves of a storm, and then patch reefs wear down the waves even more as they approach the shorelines, making them less damaging to the coast.

Irma was a category 5 hurricane that hit the lower Florida Keys in 2017. Oceanographic buoys recorded 35-foot waves just a little over five miles offshore. These enormous waves first crashed over the barrier reef and then were reduced in size as they crossed the miles of inshore patch reefs that blocked and dissipated their energy. When the waves finally made it to shore, they were 4–8 feet high, not the three-story monsters that would have demolished every single structure, including CAT 5 buildings which were built to withstand strong winds but not waves this high.

Even without a hurricane in the forecast, reefs continue their job of protecting our shorelines from rough water caused by normal winds and storms. To illustrate this, NOAA routinely provides weather service marine forecasts which are sent out to mariners, fishermen, and coastal inhabitants in the Florida Keys. They typically go something like this: "Today's forecast is for winds out of the south at 10–15 miles per hour. Waves inside the reef will be 1–2 feet and waves outside the reef will be 3–5 feet." Wait a minute! Did you hear what he just said? The reef caused the inside seas to calm down by 2–3 feet, even when the winds were not very strong.

Although out of sight, coral reefs stand as a bastion of shoreline protection. It is predicted that a loss of one meter of reef height would double annual costs from flood damage all around the world.[6] With coral reefs diminishing and sea levels rising, we will be losing this vital coastal safeguard. Perhaps in the future we will be forced to migrate inland from the coastline. In countries like the Maldives where everyone lives on island atolls, this is a daily worry, not a future concern.

Medicine Cabinets of the Sea

Coral reefs support more species per unit area than any other marine environment, including about 4,000 species of fish, 800 species of hard corals, and thousands of other species. Furthermore, scientists estimate that there may be millions of undiscovered species of organisms living in and around reefs. This biodiversity is considered key to finding new medicines for the 21st century.[7]

Biomedical researchers have been looking to the ocean and marine organisms for new natural products that could be used in medicine. And why wouldn't they? A majority of the medicines that are in use today were originally derived from terrestrial organisms and plants. The ocean is a vast wilderness of possibilities waiting to be explored for medical purposes. The term for seeking out potential medical therapeutics in nature is called *bio-prospecting*. Researchers who are bio-prospecting with various corals have had some remarkable discoveries, including:

* Metabolites derived from corals that have demonstrated significant anticancer activity.
* Products derived from corals have been shown to protect against, and even reverse, bone loss.
* Neuroprotective compounds—believed to be valuable in the treatment of Parkinson's disease—have come from corals. Some of these compounds can be used for relieving neuropathic pain as well.
* Molecules isolated from corals have been shown to greatly inhibit inflammation. They are even being tested to help fight forms of arthritis, including rheumatoid arthritis.[8]

The use of medical compounds derived from corals is still in the early stages, but there is great promise.

The value of coral reefs is measured in the enhancements they provide to the lives of people around the world. We should all say a heartfelt "thank you" to corals for contributing to the oxygen in the air that we breathe, for the three-dimensional habitat they provide to all the creatures that live on the reef (including the ones we like to eat), for adding to our economies through tourism dollars, for protecting our shorelines from all types of storms, and for offering up new opportunities for medicinal discoveries. It really is amazing to think about how much coral reefs contribute to this *Blue Planet* of ours.

Caribbean spiny lobster sheltering in crevices on a coral reef.

A mixed school of fish, primarily snapper and grunts, under the outstretched arms of elkhorn coral in the Florida Keys, USA.

Scuba diver near a coral wall on the Great Barrier Reef, Australia.

Wave breaking over a coral reef on Kwajalein Atoll in the Republic of the Marshall Islands. The structure of coral reefs can cause waves to break reducing wave energy at the shoreline that can cause flooding, shoreline erosion, and island overwash (photo by Curt Storlazzi, USGS).

*A healthy coral reef in the Tumon Bay Marine Preserve,
Guam, showing a number of different fish species
(photo by Curt Storlazzi, USGS).*

2

What Exactly Is a Coral?

WHILE MANY people are familiar with what a coral reef looks like, most do not know what a coral actually is. There are two groups of corals—the stony corals, also known as the hard corals, and the soft corals. Soft corals, like sea fans, sea plumes, and sea whips, are bendable, and resemble plants and trees. However, throughout this book, the word "coral" will refer to the reef-building corals. They are the hard (stony type) corals which produce calcium carbonate skeletons and contribute greatly to the overall reef structure. One of the most absurdly amazing characteristics of coral is that it is essentially a living rock (Image 2.1).

When I am asked, "What exactly is a coral?" I think of one of my favorite childhood games, *20 Questions.* Typically, I turn the question around and ask them: "What do you think it is: an animal, plant, microbe, or mineral?" This usually elicits bewilderment on the person's face, especially when they realize this is actually a trick question because the answer is "Yes, Yes, Yes, and Yes—all of the above!"

Without question, corals are extremely unique. There are no other organisms I know of that can be considered an

Image 2.1

The round boulder form on the right is a hard, or stony, coral called a brain coral, with several invertebrates called Christmas tree worms on top. While the colorful crowns of these worms are visible, most of their bodies are anchored in burrows they have bored into the brain coral. When startled, these worms rapidly retract into their burrows, hiding from would-be predators. On the left is the common sea fan, a soft coral that can move back and forth in the ocean currents.

animal, a plant, a microbe, and a mineral all at the same time. In essence, a coral is a small animal form called a *polyp* that looks like a tiny sea anemone. The polyp is able to create a calcium carbonate skeleton around itself (exoskeleton). It also has marine plants or algae living completely inside of it, as well as a specific community of microbes thriving completely on its outside surface. The coral head that you see on a reef, like a brain coral, is actually the creation of hundreds or even thousands of coral polyps that all live together in a colony.

My personal musings about corals that live in the "inner space" of our ocean planet are that they are strange enough that they might as well have come from "outer space." It doesn't sound so weird if you think of all the unusual pieces, parts, and combinations of diverse creatures that make up the coral life form. Nowhere else on this planet is there such an odd combination of organisms that work together as one crazy rock-like, reef-producing creature.

Symbiotic Relationships Are Key

In nature there are many examples of organisms that work together for a particular purpose or advantage. Most of these relationships are two-way (symbiotic) relationships. Symbiotic relationships include *mutualism* where both organisms benefit, *commensalism* where one benefits but the other does not, and *parasitism* where one benefits and one is harmed.

A famous example of mutualism is the clownfish and the sea anemone. This relationship was made famous in the Disney movie "Finding Nemo," and within their relationship both seem to have advantages, although we are not sure how much each requires of the other to survive. There are anemones that do exist without clownfish, in places like the Atlantic Ocean and Caribbean Sea where there are no clownfish. There are also clownfish that can be grown in captivity without anemones. In the wild however, in places where clownfish and anemones both exist—they do so in mutually beneficial harmony.

The relationship is established when a clownfish brushes up against the stinging tentacles of an anemone. The mucous from the anemone rubs off on the clownfish which then camouflages it from the anemone. The clownfish can survive this self-inflicted abuse because the reward is greater than the cost—it can now safely hide from predators among the anemone's stinging tentacles. The anemone recognizes the mucous on the outside of the clownfish and, consequently, recognizes the clownfish as part of itself.

The clownfish in return brings back bits of food to its landlord, helping to nourish its flexible housing partner. Sounds simple enough but it has its complications. Sometimes absence does not make the heart grow fonder. If the clownfish stays away for too long, the anemone does not recognize its partner anymore and stings it. The clownfish must then repeat the agonizing steps with the sea anemone to once again create the camouflage mucous coat.

Corals have symbiotic (mutualistic) relationships too. These symbiotic relationships are among the polyp itself, the algae, and the community of microbes. They all benefit greatly from each other. These relationships are essential to the health and life of the coral. Today, the scientific term *coral holobiont* is used to describe this multiple assemblage of symbiotic partners, and their fascinating relationships will be brought to light in the chapters ahead.

3

Animal: The Coral Polyp

M OST DIVERS can't help but notice and appreciate the unique shapes and spectacular colors of the coral colonies that make up any reef they approach. This includes the branching, mountainous, boulder, finger, and pillar coral colonies, to name a few—all of which help create the overall profile of a coral reef. What a diver may not notice are the individual creatures that are attached to one another in each separate colony. Each coral colony, sometimes called a *coral head*, can be made up of hundreds to thousands of these animals called *polyps* and coral polyps are the building blocks for the colonies upon which they live.

The coral polyp is classified under the animal kingdom in a phylum known as Cnidarians. The Cnidarians have other relatives you may be more familiar with, such as jellyfish or the sea anemone. They all have tentacles with stinging cells in their tips which are used primarily to capture prey. They have some similarities in appearance and can differ in size. And yes, they all look like alien life forms. Coral polyps are relatively small—much smaller than a jellyfish or sea anemone. Having very limited organ development, they are simple multicellular organisms. They have what they need to survive, however, and they do it well (see Images 3.1 and 3.2).

Image 3.1

The picture on the top is a colony of staghorn coral, a very beautiful branching coral. The photo on the bottom is a magnification of part of a staghorn coral branch. There you will see the tentacles of the polyps sticking out of their corallite homes (their exoskeleton made from calcium carbonate). Staghorn polyps are considered small and are approximately 1–2 mm in diameter. Photo credits: NOAA (top) and Anderson Blair Mayfield (bottom).

Tentacles

Polyps of reef-building corals have as a characteristic design six (or multiples of six) tentacles that surround a mouth on the end of a tube-like form. The ring of tentacles assists in capturing food, expelling waste products, and moving away debris that can accumulate on these creatures, such as sand and detritus. Specialized stinging cells called *nematocysts* are

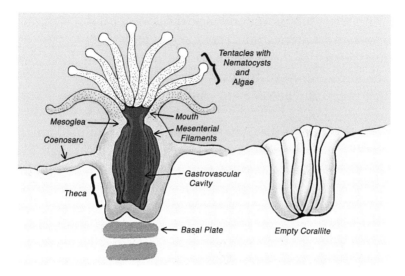

Image 3.2

An illustration of the cross section of a coral polyp identifying its basic anatomy. On the right is a cross section of the corallite, a cup-shaped home made of calcium carbonate where a polyp once lived. Each polyp creates and lives in its own corallite on the surface of a coral colony. Polyps in a colony are connected by living tissue called the coenosarc. The hard structure below the coenosarc layer is skeletal calcium carbonate. Image credit: Gwen Eyeington/Randall Scott.

located in the outer tissue and tentacles of the polyp and are used both for defense and the capture of food. They consist of a tightly bundled barb-like spear that is coiled up and ready to fire. Tiny sensors in the ends of the tentacles, stimulated either chemically or physically, trigger the nematocyst to eject. When the polyp feeds, it will sting and reel in microscopic marine creatures, such as plankton, and then move them to its mouth by way of their tentacles.

Mouth and Body

The mouth of the polyp is the opening into the flexible, tube-shaped structure that essentially is the body of the polyp.

Within this tube is a gastrovascular cavity. This simple stomach has mesenteries which are internal folds that increase the surface area of the stomach, aiding in digestion. They also contain mesenterial filaments, as well as reproductive cells that eventually become eggs and sperm (gametes) in sexual reproduction.

The mouth of the polyp is extraordinary and used for all vital life functions. Not only does food go in through the mouth, but then all waste products go back out through the same orifice. Bundles of gametes are also released through the mouth during spawning events. This may not sound very appealing to us, as humans have three different openings for these functions, but it works well for the polyp.

Outsiders Living on the Inside

Polyps live in very close association with plants and microbes, both of which are integral to its overall life and health. The plants that live in polyps are actually algae. They live inside the coral tissue (mesoglea) with higher densities of algae living in the tentacles. The polyp is a good caretaker of the algae and will extend the tentacles at various times so that the algae receive the right amount of sunlight for photosynthesis. In return the algae provide the polyp nutrition in the form of carbohydrates created during that photosynthesis process—a true symbiotic relationship. The outside layer of the polyp is the epidermis, on top of which a vital mucous layer grows. This layer envelops the outside of the coral. Within it, there are a variety of microbes (bacteria, fungi, viruses) that live and grow. These microbes help the polyp fend off disease.

The Corallite Castle

You could say the polyp's home is its castle, and fortunately each polyp has one—complete with strong walls that offer secure protection. This "castle" is called a *corallite*, a cup-like receptacle that the polyp makes and resides in. Each polyp secretes calcium carbonate to create this protective cup around itself. The "walls" of the corallite are the theca and the "floor" is the basal plate, which helps the polyp attach to the substrate. Substrate can be rock, other corals, marine debris, or any hard surface on the ocean floor. The corallite is the home of the polyp into which it can fully retreat when predators or environmental dangers threaten it. When no danger is present and conditions are favorable, the polyp will extend part of its body and all of its tentacles out of the cup to feed. The polyp will also extend when necessary to defend itself.

Identical Neighbors

Amazingly, corals start out as one individual polyp. They do not live in isolation for long and asexually reproduce neighbors by dividing or budding. The polyps will continue to reproduce asexually, increasing the size of the overall colony. This form of reproduction creates polyps in a colony that are genetically identical to each other. Polyps are joined together by a thin tissue layer called the *coenosarc*. The coenosarc connects the entire coral colony like a network and covers the underlying coral skeleton.[1]

Polyp Sizes

Coral polyps vary in size and shape depending on their species. The size of the coral polyp is interesting in that it has no bearing on the size a coral colony will grow to once mature. The colonies can all grow to be quite large.

Polyps that are considered small are about the size of the head of a pin—approximately 1–2 mm in diameter. An example of this can be seen in the branching staghorn and elkhorn corals, so named because their colonies look like deer and elk antlers respectively. These corals do a good job illustrating the lack of correlation between polyp size and the colonies they produce, as individual staghorn coral colonies can grow to 4 feet in height and 6 feet in diameter. Individual elkhorn colonies tend to be even more massive and can grow to be 6 feet in height and 12 feet in diameter. And yet they both have the smallest sized polyps of the reef-building corals. Medium-sized polyps are about 3 mm in diameter and are found in massive corals such as star corals (*Orbicella* sp). The colonies of these corals can be mountainous, forming dome-shaped mounds with uneven surfaces and bulging projections. They are termed "boulder" corals but can also be lobed. Larger coral polyps can be the size of a grape (6–12 mm in diameter), as seen in the "great star coral" (*Montastraea cavernosa*) which forms into massive boulders and sometimes develops into plates depending on water depth (see Images 3.3 and 3.4).

If we were to grow coral polyps on circular plates or plugs that are 1.25 inches in diameter (as is done in active coral restoration), they could fit between 200–300 elkhorn or staghorn polyps, 20–40 *Orbicella* sp polyps, approximately 20 brain coral polyps, and only about a dozen *Montastraea cavernosa* polyps. All of these corals can grow into very large colonies, but obviously, their polyp sizes differ dramatically.[2]

Dancing in the Dark

On the reef most coral species retract their polyps and tentacles during the day. For those lucky enough to go on a night dive, this reef world comes alive, with the polyps extending and stretching their tentacles out to try and catch passing morsels of zooplankton. This feeding response and capture behavior is something home aquarists enjoy witnessing, and they get to see this at all hours without having to worry about holding their breath, defogging their mask, or clearing their snorkel.

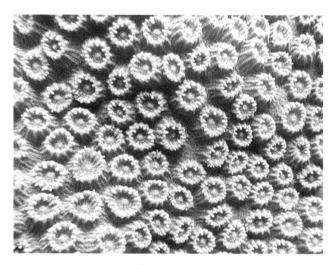

Image 3.3

Magnified polyps of boulder star coral, which are considered medium-sized polyps and are about 3 mm in diameter.

Image 3.4

Magnified polyps of the "great star coral," which can range from 6–12 mm in diameter.

4

Plant: The Algae Within

I NTERNAL FARMING is not a term you would usually asso-
ciate with corals, or really any animal for that matter. Yet,
remember, corals are part plant as well and have the ability to
essentially farm the marine plants that live inside the polyp.
Through photosynthetic activity, these marine plants (a type
of microscopic algae) provide food to the polyp in the form
of carbohydrates (sugars). If only we could internally farm
our food, then we could obtain most of our nutritional needs
from sunbathing. The following general overview of algae
helps to better understand these fascinating plants that have
the ability to live and grow inside the polyp animal.

Algae, in general, are very diverse in terms of physical size
and the pigments they contain which give them their color.
They can live in freshwater, seawater, and on wet rocks. On
land they establish mutualistic relationships with fungi to
produce lichens. Algae may be single-celled or form colonial organisms such as seaweed. They are unique from other
marine and land plants in that they do not need a specialized
organ to produce reproductive structures, such as flowers and
fruits. Instead, each algal cell has the capacity to reproduce

itself both asexually, by forming spores, and sexually through the production of gametes (sex cells). Over time they have specialized in the utilization of different pigments to capture the energy of the sun for photosynthesis. As a result, these remarkable plants have been successful for millions of years.

Green Slime and Bird Baths

Early in my career when I told some friends that I was culturing algae, their first thought was of the green slime growing in their bird bath. They told me that I could help myself to it anytime. That bird bath slime probably doesn't get the respect it deserves. If you were to put a drop of that bird bath water on a glass slide and then place it under a microscope, you would see a grand array of shapes, sizes, and colors. With the varieties of algae found in birdbaths and elsewhere, taxonomists have wrestled with how to best classify them into the scientific groupings of phyla, divisions, and classes.

The simplest nomenclature occurred when they were first identified by their photosynthetic pigments (colors) such as blue-green, brown, red, and green. Almost 2.7 billion years ago, blue-green algae were everywhere and were the first oxygen producers on the planet. Fast forward to 1.2 billion years ago, brown and red algae came on the scene, followed by green algae 750 million years ago.[1] Green algae, or Chlorophyta, are one of the most diverse groups, and members contain the green pigment chlorophyll. Chlorella is a common, single-cell green alga, and the chances of finding it in that bird bath are quite good.

Algae come in all sizes. Some are single-celled and microscopic. Multicelled strands, filaments, and more complex forms may have advanced from algae cells that divided but did not separate. There are algae that grow into large multicellular sheets or mats such as the edible sea lettuce (*Ulva*) and other easily recognized larger species of seaweeds, both obvious when they wash up on beaches. The brown algae *sargassum* start off attached to the ocean floor, but are equipped with air bladders to keep them afloat. Sargassum may eventually break off and continue to grow as floating seaweed, aggregating and forming extensive mats on the surface of the ocean. Giant kelps that resemble underwater forests are brown algae and can grow to be over 200 feet in length.[2] From single algal cells, some 500 times smaller than the head of a pin, to the large and lengthy kelp, the variation in the size of algae is enormous.

Some algae can be toxic. Many people are aware of unpleasant algae known as a *red tide*. Comprised of a special group of algae called dinoflagellates, it can grow in extreme abundance and look like a red sheen on portions of the sea. A red tide produces toxins that can kill fish and marine mammals, as well as irritate the respiratory tract of people and animals on nearby beaches.

The "Zoo" Inside the Animal

Not all dinoflagellates produce toxins, however, and a few species have adapted to live inside the coral polyp tissue. Scientists have given this type of dinoflagellate algae a special name, zooxanthellae (living inside an animal). Zooxanthellae are a specific group of algae under the genus *Symbiodinium* (and a few other genera), and they play a vital role inside the coral polyp.

Zooxanthellae have photosynthetic pigments which give corals their brilliant characteristic colors as the polyp itself is colorless (Image 4.1). More important, these pigments are the powerhouses where photosynthesis takes place. Zooxanthellae generously share their photosynthetic products of carbohydrates and oxygen with the polyp. The carbohydrates received by the polyp provide close to 90% of its energy needs.[3] In addition, they remove metabolic waste from the polyp, keeping it clean and healthy. The polyp, in return, provides the algae with a protective environment and the compounds it needs for photosynthesis and growth. Furthermore, the polyp will extend its tentacles to make sure its zooxanthellae get the sunlight they need for

Image 4.1
*These coral polyps reveal both green and orange coloring
provided by their zooxanthellae.*

photosynthesis to occur. Because this is a mutually beneficial, symbiotic relationship, the zooxanthellae are also called
the algal symbiont, or algal partner, of the polyp.

Scientists have discovered that there isn't just one single
species of zooxanthellae. They now know there are at least
nine described species with many subspecies. The numbers
of species and subspecies will change as the taxonomy of
zooxanthellae is constantly revised.[4] Here we will refer to
these subspecies, or lineages, as *clades*.

Specific types of coral polyps prefer one clade over another
and will have a higher percentage of that clade in its tissue.
These clades can differ from each other in their geographic
ranges, and how well they tolerate changes in temperature as
well as other environmental conditions. Clades can change
in the coral polyp and the methods by which they change is
one of the least understood relationships of the coral holobiont organism.

Switching and Shuffling

We do know there are two unique ways to change the amount and type of clades within the coral polyp. One is called *switching* and the other is *shuffling*. Switching relates to a coral changing out its clade of zooxanthellae over time, so a coral may have one dominant clade early in life but a different one when it is older. Shuffling refers to the many types of clades that can be changed in abundance, or diversity, and may take place within a short period of time. Just like shuffling a deck of cards if you wish to get rid of all your jacks and keep more of your aces, a coral seems to be able to shuffle out some clades and keep others.[5]

The phenomenon of switching or shuffling different clades of zooxanthellae can have great impact on the fitness and survival of the corals. It is similar to changing the type of farm seed used after a drought or freeze to enhance the chances of a better crop in the future. For corals this behavior may allow them to survive after a hot spell and/or a bleaching event by using the clade that can survive higher temperatures. Switching and shuffling are genetically important and evolutionarily critical for enhancing the chances of survival and success in the growth of corals.[6] Future scientists may have the ability to manipulate the algal symbiont by culturing the preferred species of the clades when running a hatchery. Add a little clade "D" plus a pinch of clade "A" and a smidgen of clade "B" to the mix of culture water when the coral is first taking in the algal symbionts.

While most baby corals don't come packed with the algal partners to start their farming relationship, some do. The ones who do have them already supplied by the parents that brood their coral babies inside their polyps as a form of reproduction. The others that broadcast their eggs or sperm into the water column must acquire them on their own. And this is a very critical step. It is not like they can buy them in a store or borrow some from a friend to help start their internal farm. But they do have to somehow get some successfully inside of their body tissue for their nutritional needs.

Coral biologists call the process by which corals acquire their zooxanthellae *infection*. These coral biologists were most likely coral disease specialists or microbiologists, so the word infection seemed appropriate from their perspective. If you were an aquaculture phycologist—a person who grows algae for aquaculture purposes—you would call this your *starter culture* or *inoculum*.

It is not surprising that a few different clades may get started in a young coral when this original inoculation or infection starts. Furthermore, it is not surprising that some clades can grow faster or better than others and become more populated in corals. Whether the algal growth rate, or the acceptance by the host coral, are the factors that control this—or if the coral even has the ability to monitor each clade's activities—is not well understood. What we do know is that switching can take place over time and is most likely determined by the fitness of the algae, while shuffling can be accomplished in a short period of time and is most likely controlled by the coral.

Arrivals

Little is known about how the algae actually get inside the polyp and even less about how it gets out, so more scientific research needs to be done to fully understand these mechanisms. To date what we do know is that to "get in" or become inoculated inside of the coral tissue, the zooxanthellae most likely come through the one central mouth opening, possibly ingested directly from the water containing floating algae, or picked up by the tentacles from adjacent sediments where they may have settled.

Once inside, the zooxanthellae still need to survive the digestive conditions in the gut of the polyp and not be killed in the process. Next, it must become absorbed through the tissue lining of the gut and remain alive in the inner parts of the coral. It is essential that primary polyps, the first polyps to start a coral colony after sexual reproduction, get inoculated quickly. This way they can start the internal farming process and have the energy they need to grow.

Departures and Coral Bleaching

Zooxanthellae leave the security of their home within the coral polyp in a process known as *coral bleaching*. Coral bleaching has nothing to do with Clorox, or any similar product, but describes the process of coral expelling a large percentage of its own zooxanthellae. It occurs when the ocean water warms to higher-than-normal temperatures. When it goes past a certain threshold temperature, the colorfully pigmented zooxanthellae leave the coral causing the colony to appear white or "bleached." We are seeing much more of this in recent decades with climate change, a term now well-known to the general public. To better understand coral bleaching, we need to learn what triggers the release of zooxanthellae, and then how it is actually accomplished. One theory states that it is driven by the coral polyp as a survival response under unfavorable conditions—a calculated last-ditch effort to prevent itself from imminent death or long-term starvation. It is similar to throwing your food reserve out of the life raft to prevent capsizing in a storm.

To expand this theory a bit further, the symbiotic relationship between polyp and zooxanthellae works well most of the time, but at certain times can be set on a collision course because we have an animal and a plant living so intimately together. When things do not go well, the problem is intensified since one is living inside of the other. Normally, all animals have an optimal temperature range in which they can survive and when they are out of that range, their biological systems do not function as well, if at all. When the surrounding temperature is out of the optimal range for one but not the other, things can go wrong very quickly.

High water temperatures in the summer that start approaching 90°F or 31–32°C will cause the coral polyp to be out of temperature range for its own normal metabolic processes. But plants, like trees, grass, seaweed, or single-celled algae, may grow perfectly well, or even better, in these sunlit summer months that produce higher temperatures. Under these conditions, the coral polyp may become very lethargic, while zooxanthellae continue on with photosynthetic activity, cranking out products of oxygen and carbohydrates.

Under normal conditions the polyp diffuses this excess oxygen into the surrounding water which benefits the ocean environment (and us!). However, when the polyp is lethargic or stressed from the higher water temperature, it cannot process the oxygen or transfer it out of its own polyp fast enough which could mean trouble. We usually don't think of oxygen being bad, but again, too much of a good thing can be. The excess oxygen can accumulate causing oxidative stress in the polyp tissues, leading to irreparable damage or even death.[7] But before this happens, somehow the polyp senses its demise and under some unknown process jettisons most of the algae out of its tissue. I can only imagine the anthropomorphic type of commands by the polyp being something like, "You're killing me here!" or "Ok, I have had enough, everybody out!" The coral animal then expels the algal cells out of its tissues through the mouth opening in what could be thought of in human terms as "throwing up." The polyp sacrifices its own internal algal farm and consequent nutrition as a last-ditch effort to not die of oxygen poisoning (see Image 4.2).

The results are the loss of the zooxanthellae and the continuous paling of the polyp. When 80–90% of the colorful algae have left, the polyp is considered bleached. The coral colony looks white because the coral polyp is basically clear or colorless. And just below the animal polyp is the white exoskeleton made up of calcium carbonate, which, like our own bones, is white in color. Therefore, you are looking through

Image 4.2
*In the foreground, a brain coral has lost more than
half of its zooxanthellae in the process of becoming bleached.
In the background other bleached colonies can be seen.
Photo credit: Dan Mele.*

the colorless animal and seeing what looks like a clean white form. Bleached corals can no longer gain energy from photosynthesis, and if the zooxanthellae do not return and bleaching persists for an extended period, corals will starve and die (see Image 4.3).

For those that do survive, bleaching can deplete the corals' energy resource to the extent that they do not reproduce for one or two years. The threat to corals increases as the bleaching events become more frequent because they have no time to recover.[8] In the late 1900s, we thought bleaching was just a once in a 100-year event and that over time corals would recover. In the 1970s in Florida, we had a bad bleaching event and recovery occurred. In the 1980s, we had two major bleaching events and it was obvious that this was not a once-a-century occurrence. There have been dozens of bleaching events in the last few decades and Australia has had major bleaching events more recently in 2016, 2017, 2020, and 2022.[9,10] Regretfully, these bleaching events are becoming

Image 4.3
A thicket of bleached staghorn coral colonies. Photo credit: NOAA.

commonplace, and scientists are trying to find solutions to this devastating loss of coral life.

The zooxanthellae are the critical plant component of the polyp, essential to the health and life of the coral colony. In the next chapter, the intriguing relationship between the microbial community (the other symbiotic partner) and the polyp will be explored. This dance of life between animal, plant, and microbe is fascinating.

5

Microbe: Immunity from the Outside In

IF YOU'VE ever had a gut feeling that you have something in common with corals—you were right! We are both dependent on our microbial friends to function normally.[1] Our human bodies harbor a huge array of microorganisms. While bacteria are the biggest players, we also host single-celled organisms known as archaea, as well as fungi, viruses, and other microbes.[2] Collectively, they are called our *microbiome*. While the human microbiome lives on top of and throughout our bodies, they heavily populate our gut, helping to extract nutrients from digested food. The human microbiome has been receiving more and more attention in both the scientific community and mainstream news as an indicator of overall human health.

It is now known that corals have a microbiome comprised of hundreds of thousands of microorganisms imperceptible to the human eye that are essential to their health as well. The coral microbiome (consisting of bacteria, viruses, archaea, and fungi) lives in the mucous layer that envelops the outside of the polyp. The surface of the coral colony offers many different nooks and crannies for microbes to live in. This array of microhabitats helps make corals one of the most diverse ecosystems in the world. The number and types of these bacterial communities can vary across coral species, colonies, and reefs.[3]

Both humans and corals heavily rely on their microbiomes to maintain health. The microbiome assists in the transport of nutrients, the enhancement of immune response, and the prevention of disease. When we think of an immune system, we typically think of the immune systems of higher organisms, such as ours, complete with organs, tissues, cells, and weapons against infection: spleen, liver, white blood cells, and antibodies. For corals, their microbiome functions as their entire immune system. In return, the mucous layer of the polyp provides the microbial community with a nicely protected world to live and thrive.

Hey, Whatcha Got Growing on You?

A number of studies have documented the general composition of the coral's microbial communities. Exact identifications, however, are not easy as a majority of the marine bacteria cannot be grown in a laboratory. Scientists must then rely on genetic sequence-based surveys for attempting to analyze the communities. They collect genetic material in the field using a syringe, suction off the mucous layer from a particular coral colony, and then analyze it by using DNA style forensics. This is done by first multiplying the nucleic acid material in enough volume to conduct a PCR (polymerase chain reaction) test, similar to those used for viruses.

Certain laboratories have gene banks of microbial DNA, and they will compare the DNA from the mucous sample to the DNA in their database and look for the closest match. What that really means is the entire microbiome sample suctioned off a star coral, for example, is blended to collect the DNA sequences of the microbial population. From this, gene patterns will emerge and will be compared to the gene bank. The most likely match to a microbial species, or a list of hundreds of species, then reveals the microbial members within the microbiome of that particular star coral.

It is easy to question the data resulting from such an arms-length sampling technique. Comparing the sample DNA to the DNA of known microbes, however, does give us useful information. When complementary techniques are used over time, we can gain insight into what is taking place microscopically. These surveys have shown tight associations between specific coral species and their bacterial partners. They also indicate that during normal seasonal changes of temperatures many corals show a fairly stable microbial community. Of particular interest, thousands of the bacterial sequences sampled haven't matched anything in current databases. These anonymous bacteria have not been reported in any other ecosystem and are likely to be entirely new bacterial species.[4]

Antibiotics

The bacterial species within the coral microbiome are known to produce antimicrobial and antibacterial compounds. These compounds keep other bacteria and microorganisms away, thereby keeping their own species dominant within the mucous layer. In addition, they help prevent disease and overgrowth in the immobile coral.[5] It is a perfect situation because when the bacterial community of the microbiome protects itself, it protects the surface of the coral at the same time. This essentially creates an immune barrier on the outside of the coral. Just as humans use antibiotics supplied by pharmaceutical companies to prevent non-beneficial bacteria from taking hold of us and causing infections, the same is true with the bacteria in the microbiome of the coral.

Recent studies have shown that seasonal changes in the microbial community also correlate directly with the production of these naturally occurring antibiotic compounds.[6] During normal seasonal temperatures, the mucous shows a ten-fold ability to suppress invasive microbes—including known disease pathogens—from the mucous layer of the coral.

Double Trouble

Unfortunately, the antibiotic activity of the microbiome decreases significantly during bleaching events.[7] The bleaching story discussed in the previous chapter becomes more complicated since there is a relationship between the zooxanthellae and the microbiome.

When water temperatures in the summer rise and cause coral bleaching, the nutrition provided by the zooxanthellae is greatly reduced. It turns out the nutrition the zooxanthellae provides for the coral polyp also helps to nourish the microbiome as well. Consequently, the natural immune-type system set up by the microbiome starts to collapse due to lack of nutrition from the algae. This results in a starving polyp with a compromised immune system that is more susceptible to disease. We now more fully understand the double trouble that a slight increase in water temperature can impart on corals—bleaching and disease. Coral colonies are made up of thousands of polyps, so if one polyp is affected by these conditions, then most, if not all, other polyps within the colony are suffering as well.

Epidemics

For many millennia, the symbiotic relationships between zooxanthellae, the microbiome, and the coral polyp has worked, despite occasional diseases that would eliminate a few individuals within a species. We didn't see any evidence of major epidemics until the 1970s. This could either have been because we weren't studying corals very carefully prior to this time or because times have changed. Why the sudden increase in infectious diseases among corals? Did malicious bacteria and viruses suddenly evolve to become much more lethal to corals? Maybe. But, more likely, what we're seeing is the result of a confluence of many factors, most of which humans are responsible for.

In the 1970s the first cases of *black-band disease* started to wipe out entire chunks of coral reefs (see Image 5.1). This disease is exactly what it sounds like—a black band of death stretching in swaths of disease across the surface of the coral. In the years that followed, we've seen the rise of a slew of similar diseases and names: yellow band, white band, yellow spot, and white spot, most of which spread like the black-band disease. Some of these diseases first affected corals like the staghorn and elkhorn species—the relatively fast-growing species that create a large surface area of tissue. The non-branching corals, like brain corals, dodged the early devastation by some of these diseases until just recently.

In 2014 a new disease sprung up: stony coral tissue loss disease, or SCTLD. As the name suggests, this disease works by

Image 5.1
A colony of symmetrical brain coral affected by black-band disease in the Florida Keys. Photo credit: Christina Kellogg, USGS.

killing the living polyps and connective tissue of the coral. SCTLD was first observed in South Florida near Miami and has rapidly spread both north and south. Its presence was first noted in the Caribbean in 2018 and 2019 in places like Saint Martin in the Virgin Islands and Punta Cana in the Dominican Republic. In 2020 it had finally reached the lower Keys. This disease is particularly concerning for several reasons. First, the previous diseases were mostly isolated to a few species of corals. SCTLD, on the other hand, affects over 20 of the Caribbean's reef-building corals. Second, this disease has an unusually high mortality rate, and most infected coral colonies will die within a few weeks. Last, and in part due to the massive number of species it can infect, this disease jumps from colony to colony at an alarming rate (see Image 5.2).

Image 5.2
A colony of threatened pillar coral showing advanced tissue loss due to SCTLD—a prime example of tissue loss in corals. Photo credit: Leslie Henderson, NOAA.

Home

The coral polyp depends on its microbiome and zooxanthel-lae partners to survive. One of the main benefits they receive from the polyp is a place to live. When the polyp defends itself from predators, it also is defending them. The biggest line of defense the polyp creates is the calcium carbonate exo-skeleton that it can retreat to for ultimate safety. This barrier protects the polyp, the zooxanthellae, and the microorgan-isms. This calcium carbonate home will be explored in the next chapter.

6

Mineral: Caught Between a "Rock and a Hard Place"

MANY ORGANISMS have skeletons, some on the inside (endoskeletons), some on the outside (exoskeletons), and some even leave them behind as geologic structures. Skeletal remains left behind include some of the smallest marine organisms like diatoms and coccolithophores. Diatoms are single-celled algae that produce an exoskeleton that is primarily made up of silicon. These silicon dioxide compounds are as hard as rock and when diatoms die their skeletons accumulate on the ocean floor and form huge sedimentary layers that can be hundreds of feet thick. Silicon dioxide is what all silica sand is made of and is also mined and melted to make glass products. Coccolithophores, on the other hand, have calcite exoskeletons and a large portion of the English coastline called the "White Cliffs of Dover" are made from them. Billions of them were deposited in a shallow sea above present day England almost 100 million years ago and thrust upwards due to movements of the earth's crust.[1]

Home Construction

Many mollusks, such as clams, oysters, scallops, and mussels, make their own calcium carbonate exoskeletons like corals. The structure is quite different in that the exoskeletons of mollusks consist of two shells, or valves, hinged together by a tight muscle. Because of this they are known as bivalves. Their soft bodies grow inside these protective shells which must grow with them as they mature. The growth process for expanding their two-shell home is quite interesting and we will consider the clam as an example.

A young clam, like all bivalves, is soft bodied and enclosed by two shells held together by tight muscles. When it is time to feed and respire, the clam extends an appendage called a siphon. In mollusks, siphons can be singular or paired, and their function is to pump surrounding water into and out of its body. The clam uses paired siphons like a two-way snorkel, pumping water in through one siphon and expelling water out through the other. Most bottom-dwelling clams will do this from under the sand, extending the tip of their siphon out of the sandy sediments. In addition to getting oxygenated water to pass over its gills for respiration, the clam also filters out tiny algae for its food.

As the clam eats and grows, it must also increase the size of its shell to accommodate its expanding internal body because it does not shed its old shell and grow a new one like crabs, lobsters, and shrimp. The clam (and other mollusks) adds just a little bit of shell at a time causing it to slowly grow larger and wider. It does this trick by laying down new very thin layers of calcium carbonate shell on the inside. Each day (and some-times each tide) the clam adds more to the inside of its shell. These new layers of calcium carbonate can be seen under a microscope, and sometimes with the naked eye. A thin dark band may be observed on the outside of its shell where small incremental layers were laid down in a slow-growing season, which may have been caused by a variety of environmental changes. An area of wider, lighter colored bands would be indicative of fast growth during the best part of the season with favorable environmental conditions and readily available food. Overall, one can infer a lot of information about the life history of that clam, and its environment, by looking at the shell. Just like the annular rings can tell a story about tree growth, the shells of mollusks show a history of its age and the preceding environmental conditions. Next time you walk on a beach and pick up a shell, or eat bivalves in a restaurant, you can see these layered bands if you look hard enough (Image 6.1).

Snails, whelks, and conchs are types of gastropod mollusks that live in a single spiral shell made of calcium carbonate. The shell grows as the soft bodied creature inside grows, adding to the spiral whirl as the creature within gets bigger and wider. With each increment of growth, its opening gets larger, allowing the animal to expose its body at various times to move, eat, and so forth.

Each coral polyp makes its own exoskeleton as well. A coral head is actually a colony of coral polyps that is living on the surface of the exoskeletons of previous polyps that have divided and moved upward and outward. So, the outermost surface of the coral is where all the living polyps reside. Below them are the calcium carbonate skeletons of the generations

Image 6.1
Northern quahog clam or chowder clam (left) and eastern oysters (right) are favorite seafood choices. Growth lines for both species can be seen on their outer shells. Photo credit: NOAA.

of coral polyps that existed in those positions previously. When a coral head actually dies, it leaves behind a white rock-like structure made of—you guessed it—exoskeletons (see Image 6.2).

In corals the growth sequence of the exoskeleton is slow and deliberate. It happens around the sides and underneath each polyp where it attaches itself to the substrate. The coral polyp uses calcium and the carbonate ion, both present in ocean water, and combines them to form calcium carbonate ($CaCO_3$). As a mineral compound, it can take the form of aragonite or calcite. This hard mineralization forms the coral exoskeleton that resembles a "cup" where each polyp resides. This cup-shaped structure is the corallite that was discussed in Chapter 3. The intricate inner surface of the corallite is the calyx, and the accumulated residual that eventually forms underneath becomes the reef itself.

DISCLAIMER IF CHEMISTRY GIVES YOU HEADACHES

It is difficult to explain what is going on in our oceans and on our reefs without touching on the basic chemical reactions that are taking place. So, in a few parts of this book the chemistry of climate change is discussed as briefly as possible and in general terms. This can still be confusing for some, but please don't get flustered—there is no test or exam. It is my hope that after finishing the book you will have a general understanding of what is happening and what is at stake.

The Evil Twin

The exoskeletons of coral polyps are sturdy, and some have survived for billions of years. However, they are now being threatened by the "evil twin" of climate change, *ocean acidification* (OA). We have already discussed that excess carbon

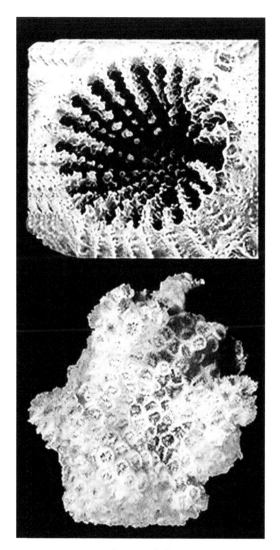

Image 6.2

The bottom image is the skeleton of an entire colony of Astrangia sp. The top image is the corallite that an individual polyp made and lived in during its life. The polyp could retract into the corallite for protection and rest and then extend its tentacles out, and sometimes its body, to feed and gather light for its zooxanthellae. Photo credit: Stephen Cairns and Marcelo Kitahara (https://creativecommons.org/licenses/by/3.0/deed.en).

dioxide (CO_2) can cause temperatures to rise in both the atmosphere and ocean, causing corals to bleach. In addition, the underwater dissolving of CO_2 adds insult to injury by changing the chemical makeup of our oceans and making seawater more acidic.

Oceans typically absorb about 30% of the CO_2 that is released into the atmosphere, while land plants take up the rest. Our global output of CO_2 from fossil fuels has been increasing steadily since the industrial revolution. There is now more carbon dioxide in the atmosphere than any time in the past 15 million years.[2] So, as atmospheric CO_2 levels increase, so does the amount of CO_2 dissolving into the ocean—approximately 30% of whatever there is in the atmosphere. You might think that because our oceans are so vast that they can absorb the excess CO_2 without much consequence, but that is not the case.

How does excess CO_2 entering our oceans actually cause ocean acidification? To answer this, we first need to consider *pH*, which is strictly defined as the negative log of the hydrogen ion concentration. The measurement scale is logarithmic so a change from 8.0 to 7.9 is a ten-fold change. The scale goes from 0–14, with readings below 7 considered acidic and readings over 7 considered alkaline (or basic). A pH measurement of exactly 7 means neutral—neither acidic nor alkaline, as seen in distilled water. Our oceans, historically, have been a little alkaline at 8.3 because of dissolved elements such as calcium, magnesium, etc. Now, the oceans near shore are starting to have pH readings of 8.1 and 8.2 indicating that the ocean, while still alkaline, is moving towards becoming more acidic. The excess of hydrogen ions is driving this trend, but how?

The Theft of Carbonate Ions

Ocean acidification occurs when excess carbon dioxide dissolves in ocean water. Carbon dioxide + water yields carbonic acid. Carbonic acid further dissociates to bicarbonate ion (HCO_3^-), which then dissociates to the carbonate ion (CO_3^{2-}). Each step of this process yields positively charged hydrogen atoms, shown in the following equation.

$$CO_2 + H_2O \leftrightarrow H_2CO_3 \leftrightarrow H^+ + HCO_3^- \leftrightarrow 2H^+ + CO_3^{2-}$$

Carbon Dioxide + Water ↔ Carbonic Acid ↔ Hydrogen ion + Bicarbonate ↔ 2 Hydrogen ions + Carbonate

Remembering that pH is measured by the negative log of the positively charged hydrogen ion, the higher the amount of hydrogen ions, the lower the PH, and the more acidic the solution. So at its core, the issue of OA is simple chemistry.[3]

Basically, as oceans become more acidic the number of positively charged hydrogen molecules increase in the seawater. Polyps of reef rebuilding corals make their exoskeletons from carbonate ions and calcium ions found in the ocean water. The polyp will bring this water into a calcifying space between its tissues and the surface of the existing exoskeleton.[4] It uses energy to pump out the excess hydrogen ions, as these ions want to bind with the carbonate ion as well, essentially competing with the calcium for the carbonate ion. Unfortunately, OA causes the overall amount of calcium carbonate in the seawater to fall because the carbonate ions that normally pair with the calcium ions prefer (chemically speaking) to pair with the hydrogen ions to make bicarbonate. Consequently, excess hydrogen ions from OA tend to keep the carbonate ions bound up. The coral polyp can pump out hydrogen ions from its calcifying space all it wants, but much of the previously available carbonate is already bound to the hydrogen. Problems now arise for the polyp because it cannot extract the carbonate ion it needs, preventing it from growing and rebuilding its exoskeleton.[5] Furthermore, unbound hydrogen ions will slowly break apart calcium carbonate in existing exoskeletons in order to steal the carbonate ions for themselves.

For coral polyps, this pH change of the ocean means their individual protective exoskeletons become weaker and in disrepair, leaving them more susceptible to predation and disease. For the coral reef as a whole, the entire structure can weaken and dissolve, harming all the creatures that depend on the reef habitat.

The chemical equation on the previous page contains back and forth arrows that signify that the compounds can change back and forth, from one form to another. In this equation, the movement is known as buffering, or a buffer system. In short, a buffer system is a solution that resists a change in pH when acids or bases are added to it (there are even three buffer systems in our human bodies). I vividly remember my college chemistry teacher trying to explain the workings of a buffer system. At the time he stated that a good example was the calcium and carbonate buffer system that helps to stabilize pH in the ocean. He added, "because of that buffer system, we could never dump enough acid into the oceans to ever change the pH." Unfortunately, that statement turned out to be false as we have done just that—not by lining up thousands of dump trucks on the coastline to send mass volumes of liquid acid into our oceans, but by burning hydrocarbons in the form of fossil fuels.

Homes that Dissolve and Disappear

Ocean acidification is not only a problem for the corals but for the many marine creatures that depend on calcium carbonate to create their shells—clams, oysters, mussels, scallops, conch, crabs, lobsters, shrimp, etc. Imagine a large chowder clam using the bulk of its energy to pump out hydrogen ions, leaving little to nothing in reserve to thicken its shell. "Thin skinned" is not a sought-after survival trait within the clam community.

All shellfish start life as a small larval form with a tiny larval shell made from calcium carbonate. These thin and literally transparent larval shells are critical for their survival, helping them to become juveniles that eventually grow up to become shellfish for your dining pleasure. Recently, because of ocean acidification, oyster growers in the northwest U.S. have had to grow their larvae inside in land-based hatcheries, adjusting the pH of the waters that the larvae are grown in so they will survive. All the tiny marine zooplankton that have calcium carbonate shells are also at risk. Because of OA they are in danger of not producing the biomass that feeds krill, fish, whales, and everything else up the food chain that depend on them.

For corals, OA requires them to use more energy to pump out excess hydrogen ions in their calcifying space, so they are not available to compete for the carbonate ion. They can expend a lot of energy doing this, energy that could be used for other processes, and still they are not always successful. Unfortunately, excess hydrogen ions can also steal carbonate ions right off the reef structure causing the reef to slowly dissolve. In some unique places where CO_2 naturally bubbles up from underwater volcanic activity, we can get a glimpse of what the future may become. The impact of pH is so bad in these few specific areas that coral exoskeletons are dissolving right out from under and around them. These shapes (think stand-alone ice cream cones) are caused by the erosion of the calcium carbonate. In some laboratory experiments, coral exoskeletons have been completely dissolved by using much lower pH levels, leaving a cluster of "naked" polyps without any skeletal structure left at all. But these of course would not survive in the natural environment as predation would be almost immediate.

CONNECTING THE DOTS

Imagine you are a coral and the water you live in was becoming warmer, too warm for you to function properly. You had to kick your zooxanthellae friends out because the excess oxygen

continued

they were producing was damaging your tissue. With them gone, however, you start to starve as they provided a lot of your nutrition. So, there you are starving and lethargic, and lo and behold your microbiome starts to change too. Your microbe friends that lived on your body surface are being affected by the warmer water temperatures because once the zooxanthellae left, part of their food source was gone as well. The microbes that kept you free from disease are becoming sickly and over-run by unwelcome, bully microbes, causing you to become even sicker. The excessive CO_2 from the air is dissolving in the water you live in, and you start to notice your calcium carbonate skeleton slowly dissolving because of the increase in ocean acidity. This is the plight of our crucially important coral in the 21st century!

The short story above illustrates the many hurdles that corals are currently facing for survival. The situation is dire. There is, however, hope. As you will see in several forthcoming chapters, there are ways to work with corals to help them survive in these changing and challenging times.

7

Coral Growth, the Odyssey from Larvae to Reef

W E HAVE learned up to this point that a coral is a small marine animal polyp with symbiotic partners made up of algae and microbes, all living inside a corallite cup. But how does this one individual coral become a coral colony? How do coral colonies then grow to build coral reefs? To understand this, we need to start at the very beginning, at reproduction itself.

Corals procreate through both sexual and asexual reproduction. Coral sexual reproduction is extremely interesting and is covered in Chapters 9 and 10. Without asexual reproduction, however, there would be no coral colonies—just individual polyps scattered here and there. The individual coral larvae, created from sexual reproduction, actually starts the coral colony. The way a coral larvae grows, through asexual reproduction into the magnificent multidimensional coral structure most people are familiar with, is quite an odyssey.

Initially, the free-swimming larval form settles on submerged rocks or other hard surfaces along the ocean floor, close to the coastlines of islands and continents. Once settled, the larva will physically change from a balloon-like form to the first primary polyp. At this stage it is tiny, fleshy, and vulnerable to predation. If not eaten first, the primary polyp will consume carbohydrates provided by the zooxanthellae that live inside of it. The polyp will also start to capture and eat plankton and to feed itself. The stream of nourishment from the carbohydrates and the plankton allows it to grow into an adult-sized polyp. At this point it is still the primary polyp, but now large enough to divide by binary *fission* or *budding*, creating two identical creatures.

Cloning the Colony

Whether a polyp divides by fission or budding depends on both the species of coral and its position within the colony. Fission occurs when a polyp divides into two identical-sized polyps. After a polyp splits in two, each one quickly grows back to the same size as the original polyp. This is where things gets cozy because technically they are in one coral-lite, and now they need two. Consequently, there comes a point during fission where each polyp starts producing more calcium carbonate to expand and then divide the corallite, so when fission is completed each polyp will have its own structural home.

During budding, a polyp will form, or *bud,* from the side of the original polyp and will also secrete calcium carbon-ate to create its own corallite. The polyp that budded is then identical to the polyp it came from. Whether created through fission or budding, the new polyp is genetically identical to the original polyp and therefore a clone.

Either way, there are now two polyps in the colony that will in turn generate even more polyps through asexual repro-duction. This gets more dramatic as you get beyond the first primary polyp split and start talking about multiple polyps in a colony. As this process continues, the small colony starts to get wider. It also starts to grow upwards and outwards into shapes that are characteristic of their particular species. The growing colony creates a stronger, more secure environment for all the individual polyps to live.

Life Is Always on the Surface

All coral polyps need to be on the surface layer to survive. Their zooxanthellae need light for photosynthesis and the polyp must be able to extend its tentacles into the water to feed. For all polyps to remain on the surface, lateral (sideways) expansion seems simple enough. There comes a point, though, when the colony needs to grow upwards in a more vertical direction. A coral polyp will periodically do this by lifting off its base and secreting a new calcium carbonate basal plate above the old one, creating a small chamber in the skeleton.[1] Once secure on the new basal plate, it will add height to the walls (theca) that surround it.

A cross section of a coral colony skeleton shows tubes of empty, connected, sealed-off corallite chambers that lead to the surface. After fission or budding, the new polyp will be next to the originating polyp but will not have this tube of chambers directly below it. It will eventually form one, however, as it divides and moves upwards (see Image 7.1).

So, the coral polyps you see on the surface of a colony are literally standing on the shoulders of their own previous exoskeletons and those of other polyps. It is interesting that the polyps themselves remain the same size but the colony itself grows by adding more polyps. This is somewhat similar to a beehive. The beehive grows, but the bees don't grow larger, they only grow larger in the number of bees. A coral colony will grow larger due to the number of polyps, but the polyp itself never grows beyond the size of the primary polyp when it made its first division. Everything beneath the living surface layer is the skeletal remains of polyp neighborhoods. The polyps grow and expand simultaneously and in slow motion relative to our sense of time. The logistics of this growth process differs a bit depending on the type of coral.

Image 7.1

On the left is the skeleton of a coral colony in the Florida Keys. It was cut several times—unevenly—when mined. Upon close inspection you can see the vertical tubes within it created by individual polyps, dividing and growing the colony as they moved towards the surface. On the right is a photo of the top of the colony showing the opening to the corallites where the polyps lived on the surface.

Branching Coral Growth

For the branching corals (e.g., staghorn and elkhorn corals), growth is somewhat similar to plant growth. New polyps near the tip of a branch will grow up and out, but only to the limits of the thickness of the branch itself. They are actually growing at the terminal tips, similar to the upward growth of vascular plants or the end branches of a hardwood tree. Currently, scientists think of branching corals as "fast-growing" corals because they can grow a few millimeters a week (the size of a pinhead or two). Consequently, branching corals can add 10 inches to their branches in one year.[2]

Branching corals do not have secondary growth like hardwood trees, which allow their limbs and trunk to get thicker. For branching corals, they can grow longer on the tips, and they can make new branch offshoots, but there are no secondary thickenings. This is what ultimately limits the size of many of the branching corals, but not all. Elkhorn coral can get wider and therefore can also get bigger.

The polyps at the tip of branching corals grow so fast that the corallite of each polyp shows more of the white-colored calcium skeleton than the pigmented coral polyp tissue. Therefore, a healthy fast-growing tip of a staghorn or elkhorn coral appears whiter in color. Many novice divers mistakenly think this new growth is a disease or bleaching on these corals when it actually is a sign of good health and growth.

Boulder Coral Growth

For the more massive corals that look like boulders, the growth expansion of the polyps—and thus the colony as a whole—is more intriguing. These types of colonies are more spherical in shape and grow not only wider but taller, all at the same time. This expansion is similar to a balloon that grows in length, width, and height as it is inflated. This expansive growth process helps create the space needed to accommodate the growing number of polyps. Scientific literature documents that these more massive corals take somewhere between a month and a year to grow a few millimeters. That yields lateral extension growth for the brain or boulder corals at only one tenth to one hundredth the rate of the branching corals.[3]

The Variety of Coral Colony Shapes

The shapes of coral colonies can be very diverse depending on the location and environment where they grow. To date, almost 800 species of reef-building corals have been identified, with new discoveries occurring each year. Of the known species, a majority are found in the Indian and Pacific Oceans.[4] We have up to this point discussed branching and boulder corals primarily because they are common to reefs worldwide and have been successfully used in current reef restoration activities. But there are many different coral shapes and forms specific to particular species of coral.

Coral species can be grouped by their basic form or structure, such as branching, pillar, massive, brain, encrusting, leaf, plate, sheet, fleshy, flower, and cup corals, to name a few.[5] There can be some variety in appearance within these groupings or categories—even among members of the same genus. For example, elkhorn coral (*Acropora palmata*) and staghorn coral (*Acropora cervicornis*) are both branching corals of the same genus, but they look quite different. The genus Porites has a variety of species ranging from large boulder coral heads to some species with small finger-like branches.

Although there are no hard and fast rules, a general description of colony shapes is very helpful in the identification of corals. We touched upon this taxonomy earlier in our discussion of polyps, but here you'll find those now-familiar species among others as we focus our attention to the colonies:

- **Branching corals** are one of the most recognized because they form branches that can range in appearance and size. Some look like antlers or fingers, and they can form dense thickets while covering large areas of the reef. They were fairly abundant a few decades ago in the Atlantic and Caribbean with staghorn and elkhorn corals populating large areas. Now they are harder to find. In the Pacific and Indian Oceans, branching corals dominate the reefscape with colonies of many beautiful colors and minor shape variations covering much of the reef area (see Image 7.2).

- **Pillar corals** are found in the western Atlantic Ocean and the Caribbean Sea. These corals can resemble clusters of cigars, or pipe organs narrowing at the top. They grow up from the sea floor and can become quite large (see Image 7.3). Pillar coral is also listed as threatened

Image 7.2
A dense thicket of staghorn coral located in the Banda Islands, Indonesia. Photo credit: Anderson Blair Mayfield.

Image 7.3
The author next to a pillar coral in the Dominican Republic.

under the Endangered Species Act and is sometimes referred to as the "unicorn" from both its shape and its potential to become extinct.[6]

* **Massive corals** are round or boulder-like in shape. They can be referred to as mountainous corals as well due to their tendency to become very large (see Image 7.4). They are impressive in size and responsible for building major portions of coral reefs. They also soften waves, protecting shorelines. Because of their size and weight, these massive corals are seldom damaged even by strong wave action.

* **Brain corals** are considered massive corals too, but because they are so unique they deserve a section of their own (see Image 7.5). These corals are interesting and easily recognized because they are roundish in shape, have grooves, and—as their name suggests—look like a human brain. The polyps of brain corals arrange themselves in a way that creates these grooves and allows for them to have common mouths every half inch or so. Brain corals can grow very large as well. When massive corals are combined with brain corals, the resulting reef colonies can be very diverse in size, shape, and color.

* **Encrusting corals** grow as a thin layer that adhere to hard or rocky surfaces (see Image 7.6). Although just attaching to the surface may seem like a minor role in the overall reef structure, it really isn't. Encrusting corals are sometimes referred to as the *cement of the reef*, binding the spaces between larger coral heads and stabilizing the rest of the reef. Encrusting corals have varied colors and surface textures.[7]

* **Leaf, plate,** or **sheet** corals can have broad plate-like portions that rise in whorl-like patterns (see Images 7.7–7.9). They form beautiful structures that have been compared to the open petals of a flower. Some look like plates that have fallen out of a perfectly stacked

Image 7.4
The author next to a massive, mountainous colony of
Porites sp. in the Maldives.

Image 7.5
A large brain coral in the Dry Tortugas, Florida. Photo credit: NOAA.

Image 7.6
An encrusting coral growing over a reef structure. The low profile of encrusting corals makes them very secure and hard to break during rough ocean conditions. Photo credit: NOAA.

arrangement, overlapping here and there. Because they can grow at depths where sunlight wanes, there are some branching corals species that grow outwards instead of upwards creating more surface area to gather the sun's rays. When they grow laterally like this they are referred to as sheet or table corals.

* **Fleshy, flower,** and **cup** corals contain many species with diverse descriptions, but are not as abundant. They are usually fleshy forms and appear to be growing out of their skeletons. They can be very ornate and look like a flower. Cup corals are solitary corals with large fleshy polyps. In all there are dozens of species and types in the Atlantic, and hundreds of species in the Pacific and Indian Oceans, with various forms, shapes,

Image 7.7
These plating corals are found 130–164 feet deep in the Flower Garden Banks National Marine Sanctuary in the Gulf of Mexico. Photo credit: NOAA.

Image 7.8
Acropora sp. located in the Spermonde Archipelago, Indonesia. Notice they are not branching up, but instead are growing laterally to form table-like structures on a short pedestal base. Some corals grow this way at depth to maximize the surface area in which it can gather the sun's rays. Photo credit: Anderson Blair Mayfield.

and sizes to match. This is what makes the coral reef so wonderful—the diverse colors, shapes, and sizes of the structures these organisms build (see Image 7.10).

The Structural Variety of Coral Reefs

Coral polyps in a colony grow in number, expanding the size of the coral colony. Colonial hard corals can consist of hundreds, to hundreds of thousands, of individual polyps.[8] As individual coral colonies grow, the coral reef community as a whole grows upward and outward as well. Corals tend to grow towards the light, similar to how trees compete for light in a forest, although the growth rate of corals is much slower. With growth rates of 0.3 to 2 centimeters per year for massive corals, and up to 10 centimeters per year for branching corals, it can take up to 10,000 years for a coral reef to form from a group of larvae.[9] As the colonies within the coral reef grow larger, the coral reef itself expands and some coral reefs may reach for miles unobstructed. Some coral colonies will grow continually along the reef for quite a distance without disconnection.

Reef-building corals prefer clear and shallow water where lots of sunlight filters through to their symbiotic algae. For this reason, they are generally found at depths less than 150 feet.[10] Coral species grow individual colonies of various shapes and sizes and the actual reefs they collectively create can take on distinct forms as well. There are a few forms or types of reefs depending on their shape and location—some say three and some believe as many as five types. I'll review the five and let you decide the official number and where you stand in the debate of which ones might be subsets of others.

Fringing Reefs

Fringing reefs are among the most common types of coral reefs. These reefs can be connected in parts to the shoreline. Sometimes they are further away from shore and create a nice lagoon between the reef and the shoreline. Fringing reefs grow

Image 7.9
A majestic reef in the Banda Islands, Indonesia. This area is dominated by corals exhibiting foliaceous, or leafy, growth forms. Photo credit: Anderson Blair Mayfield.

Image 7.10
A fleshy coral colony on a Wakatobi, Indonesia, coral reef.

upward towards the water's surface and form a reef slope as they grow out towards the sea. Many people have snorkeled or dove these types of reefs as they are found around most tropical islands and are easily accessible from the beach. They can extend from the shallowest inshore depths where wave action and tidal exposure becomes the limiting factor, to the deeper extent of the ocean slopes where they are only limited by their access to light. In certain parts of the world, fringing reefs tend to form along volcanoes due to their shallow, sloped walls. This environment makes for ideal formation conditions. The best place to find fringing reefs are in Israel, parts of the African shore, and Australia.[11]

Patch Reefs

Patch reefs are small, isolated areas of living coral surrounded and separated by sand rings and sea grasses. Typically, they are nearshore between fringing reefs and barrier reefs. Patch reefs vary greatly in size, and they rarely reach the surface of the water.[12] From the air they look like numerous dark areas or "patches" in shallow white areas of sand. The areas around patch reefs include sand bottom, sea grass, and sponge beds. The combination of these adjacent areas together with patch reefs make for a very diverse habitat for many fish and invertebrates. They are used as nurseries, feeding grounds, and places to hide from large predators—a smorgasbord of habitats for all life stages.

Barrier Reefs

Barrier reefs are probably the most well-known formation, primarily because of the Great Barrier Reef in Australia. This barrier reef is the biggest of all reefs, measuring over a thousand miles long and several miles wide. Barrier reefs in general are similar to fringing reefs in that they are also found parallel to the shore, but further out to sea. These reefs can be a few miles offshore and are usually quite extensive. Barrier reefs are separated from land by an expanse of water—creating extensive flats or lagoons between the reef and the coastline. In their shallowest areas, these reefs can reach the water's surface creating a "barrier" to navigation. The Florida reef tract in the Atlantic Ocean and the Meso-American reef tract in the western Caribbean form the next largest examples of barrier reefs.

Bank Reefs

Bank reefs are essentially built-up portions, or isolated sections, of a barrier reef. They could also be considered *a patch reef on steroids*. They are significantly larger and located further out to sea than the patch reefs of the nearshore environment. Spur and groove reefs could be considered a bank reef, or a section of barrier reef, although their reef structures (spurs) are perpendicular to the shoreline, not parallel. The spurs are coral mounds or clusters arranged with sandy spaces or *grooves* in between. The grooves allow for some waves and surges of water to flow through the reef while the spurs act as a barrier to soften the waves—protecting the flats behind them.

On the seaward side of a spur and groove reef is a slope that reaches optimal depths for diverse collections of branching and massive corals extending deeper on the open ocean edge. These types of reefs offer great diving opportunities for tourism. They also provide storm protection by allowing water to flow through sections of the reef rather than around it. The Florida Keys reef tract is composed of over a dozen smaller sections of its barrier reef, called bank reefs, that are visited by hundreds of thousands of snorkelers and divers each year.

Atolls

Atolls are famous for their circular, oval, and even horseshoe shapes. The formation is the evolutionary result of the subsidence (sinking) of islands or volcanos. What remains is the fringing coral reef that formed the rim to the now-sunken mass it once surrounded. Over time, the area where the island was becomes a lagoon that is protected from wave action. When there is a break in the fringing reef, ocean water can flush the lagoon creating conditions for many types of coral to comfortably grow. The shallowest portions of the fringing reef can become land, which is sand created from exposed coral.

The rate of atoll formation can be increased by sea level rise. The corals of the fringing reef continue to grow upward, keeping pace with the rising sea as the island or volcano within sinks faster. Atolls, with their unique environments, have become favorite dive locations. Their protected inner lagoons can be excellent safety zones for boats. Some atolls are inhabited by humans along emergent upland areas taking advantage of these unique environments.

The Perspective from Space

The various types of formations just described show the diverse ways these tiny coral animals grow and create the amazing structures we call coral reefs. Some are so large that they can be seen from space! Sometimes it takes one giant step out to the International Space Station (ISS) to see what we cannot fully comprehend. Almost every astronaut looking back at this blue ocean planet comes away with awe and reverence. In her book, *Back to Earth: What Life in Space Taught Me About Our Planet and Our Mission To Protect It*, Astronaut Nicole Stott wrote:

> *"It's probably no surprise that any astronaut's favorite use of free time in space (mine included) was floating in front of a window in awe of the stunning view of Earth below. The image of Earth viewed from space as a glowing ball of blue floating against a backdrop of blackness reminded me how special it was to be living in such a unique environment. I was captivated by the iridescent mix of blues and turquoises that swirled below and would lose track of time as I floated*

above the window with my camera and a large zoom lens aimed towards Earth. I snapped photo after photo in an effort to capture images of the ocean's beautiful, delicate patterns of coral reef structures that stretch around and dot the planet—so vivid they would stand out to the naked eye and many that stretch on for miles and miles."[13]

Stott was particularly enamored with the reef off of Venezuela, appreciating its vivid colors and pronounced formation. She marveled at how the curve of Los Roques, the coral-built archipelago, took the shape of an ocean wave. In fact, this reef was her first painting in space (see Images 7.11 and 7.12).

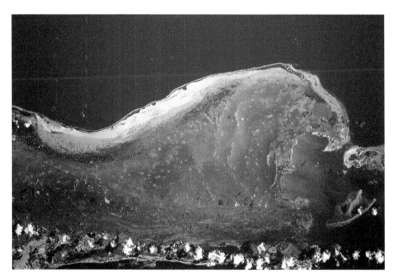

Image 7.11

Nicole took this photo while on board the International Space Station. It is the eastern portion of the Los Roques Archipelago, which is considered an extensive coral atoll off the northern coast of Venezuela. You can see fringing reefs running along the slender swirling islands and patch reefs dotting the ocean floor between them. It looked to her like someone had reached down with a big paintbrush and painted a wave on the ocean. Photo credit: Nicole Stott.

Image 7.12

The Wave—the first watercolor painting in space. Inspired by the photo on the previous page, Nicole painted her interpretation of the Los Roques Archipelago while she was still on board the ISS. Imagine trying to paint in space with liquid paint in zero gravity! Photo credit: Nicole Stott.

This sense of wonder experienced by astronauts can be similar to what divers feel in the "inner-space" of our oceans. There have been over 28 million divers certified by PADI (Professional Association of Dive Instructors) since 1967.[14] That means that millions of people have experienced the inner-space world and many of these on a coral reef. About 2 million visitors a year go to the Great Barrier Reef, a reef that can be seen from space. It is truly amazing to think that various species of microscopic coral larvae grew into a living reef that covers an area of over 133,000 square miles.

PART II

Sex, War, and Rocks that Don't Roll

8

The Fossil Record—How Fast Is the Slow Growth of Coral?

THE QUESTION of how fast or slow corals grow depends on who you ask. For many years, the study of corals has been competitively shared between two distinct groups of scientists—marine biologists and geologists. The heart of this friendly debate is whether corals are living organisms that happen to make rock skeletons or rock skeletons that happened to have been made by living organisms.

A marine biologist will compare coral growth rates to other faster growing organisms that exist today and therefore conclude that corals grow very slowly. Geologists tend to think that corals grow relatively quickly. This is because the perspective of geologists is somewhat different in that they view life through the lens of historical eras that are counted in hundreds of thousands, or even millions, of years. For example, "recent times" from a biologist's viewpoint occurred in the last 15,000 years, which is the age of most living portions of reefs today. For geologists, "recent times" include the 150,000-year-old recent fossil reef known as the Florida Keys (the island chain people live on). In addition, biologists will talk in millimeters or inches of live reef growth per year, while geologists look at miles of reef and thickness in meters when discussing reef rock.

The production of calcium carbonate rock by coral polyps not only creates a pretty reef but a habitat with variable shapes and texture. Over time, coral reefs provide the structure for the buildup of islands, the extension of new land masses, the creation of atolls, and the inland remains of coral reefs from long ago. These old ocean deposits provide some of the largest concentrations of carbonate rock, also known as limestone, quarried for making building blocks and mined for various minerals and compounds. From this perspective, ancient inland coral reefs are a treasure trove of structural materials and certain chemical elements, preserved for the taking.

Gifts to Humanity

Early humans mined this carbonate rock, which was soft enough to cut and carve while also being strong enough to bear very heavy loads. Many civilizations learned that these carbonate layers could be harvested with their simple tools and then used for a variety of structures as seen in the Mayan and Aztec pyramids, roads, and buildings. Today, if you look closely at limestone roads or building blocks you may see the tell-tale signs of a coral skeleton pattern, mixed in with other calcium carbonate skeletons like the shells of mollusks, deposited in accumulated sediments which over time and pressure became this valuable rock layer.

The remains of ancient coral reefs not only provide us with materials used in human civilization, they allow us to investigate the past. Fossilized corals provide geological indications of their biological populations and can also show how the coral reefs grew in the past, how sea level changes affected them, and how atolls and islands were formed. Fossilized corals are found almost everywhere and even hundreds of miles inland on the terrestrial part of the Earth. They are found in places like the Grand Canyon and the Great Lakes, which help illustrate how they and other marine organisms have played a critical role in the history of our planet where ancient seas were once found. If you ever have the chance to see a quarry that mined calcium carbonate rock, you can actually see the history "written in stone."

One beautiful example of fossilized coral used in jewelry, and proof of the past history of the oceans, is the Petoskey stone (see Image 8.1). My wife, Donna, wears one on a necklace as a reminder of corals past. Petoskey stone is composed of a fossilized colonial coral, *Hexagonaria percarinata*. Such stones were formed from fossilized skeletons that were originally deposited during the Devonian period in what is now

Image 8.1
A Petoskey stone on a centimeter scale showing fossilized, six-sided polyp formations.

Michigan. When dry, the stone resembles ordinary limestone, but when wet or polished the distinctive mottled pattern of the six-sided coral fossil emerges. It is sometimes made into decorative objects. The stone was named for an Ottawa chief (Pet-O-Sega), the son of a fur trader. The city of Petoskey, Michigan, is also named after him, and it is the center of the area where the stones are found. In 1965, Petoskey stone was named the state stone of Michigan.[1]

Not Just Another Brick in the Wall

The Windley Key Fossil Reef Geological State Park in the Florida Keys contains the original quarry from where much of the rock was taken to connect many of the islands, or keys, in this coral island archipelago. This quarry was used by Henry Flagler in the early 1900s to help build the Overseas Railroad through Florida and as far south as Key West. Bridge after bridge was constructed to create the first connection from mainland Florida to Key West, 42 bridges in all. The building of these bridges required cement and many tons of rock made by corals a hundred thousand years ago. Within this quarry, coral rock was cut to make structural components for the approaches to the bridges including one of the several wonders of the construction world—the Seven Mile Bridge that connects Marathon Key to Ohio Key.

What remains as a wall in this park, after the blocks were cut and moved away, is a picture board of the corals that lived long ago (see Image 8.2). As an actual slice of time, these coral skeletons show the upward and outward growth patterns as the coral heads grew and the reef filled in over thousands of years. If lucky, you may spot the single skeleton that started each coral colony sitting on the bottom of a fan like expansion of the coral itself. Upon closer inspection, you can see different types of corals, how they filled in the reef, and then eventually how they grew over the top of the reef on the shoulders of thousand-year-old giants. All of this ancient creation is from a collection of miniscule, fleshy polyps that

Image 8.2
Fossilized brain coral at Windley Key Fossil Reef Geological State Park.

lived and grew in a coordinated effort, eventually leaving behind their skeletal past. It seems almost ironic that these coral skeletons became the building blocks which makes travel through the Keys possible without ever having to get into a boat or physically touch the water at all.

Water, Ice, and Coral Reefs

Relatively speaking, coral reefs add new ground fairly quickly compared to the formation of new soil in forests, wetlands, or the accumulation of sediments which create the ocean floor. But why do we find the remains of coral reefs far inland? To better understand why these ancient coral reefs are found where they are, we need to consider the formation of land masses and the rise or lowering of sea levels over a long period of time. Here, we will focus on just the relative change of sea levels.

The one factor that greatly influences sea levels on the planet is the proportion of the Earth's water that is in the form of ice at any point in time. Not the cumulative effect of ice cubes in homes, bars, and restaurants, but ice reserves found in the North and South Poles, in glaciers, and in ice sheets that sit on top of large land masses in very cold areas such as Greenland. Generally speaking, higher global temperatures can incrementally melt these ice reserves into the sea, increasing the volume of sea water, which then causes sea levels to rise. This can be rapid depending on the speed of the temperature change. Conversely, during cold periods, snow and ice accumulate back onto the polar areas, glaciers form, and sea levels lower. This process is relatively slow as the compression of accumulated snow into ice and glaciers can take many decades.

Factors that cause changes in global temperature over time include the raising or lowering of greenhouse gases, such as carbon dioxide (CO_2), which can trap heat inside our atmosphere. Image 8.3 shows four ice age cycles and how atmospheric CO_2, global temperature, and sea level appear to be synchronized from 400,000 years ago to present day. CO_2 from the air is soluble in water, and it will move back and forth between air and water as a natural process. CO_2 prefers cooler water, and the cooler the water is, the more soluble the CO_2. Because CO_2 behaves this way, scientists are able to determine how much of it was in the atmosphere during these periods using ice core samples. Notice the amazing correlation in this graph—CO_2, air temperature, and sea level all rise and fall together.

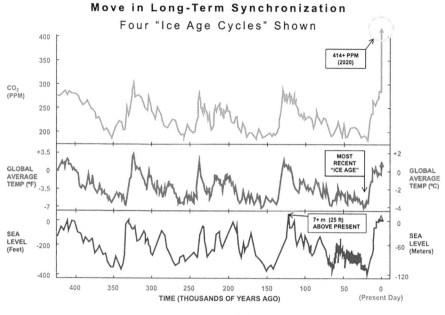

Carbon Dioxide (CO₂), Temperature, & Sea Level
Move in Long-Term Synchronization
Four "Ice Age Cycles" Shown

Image 8.3

CO_2, air temperature, and sea level synchronization. Graph is courtesy of John Englander (www.johnenglander.net) and is adapted from the work of Drs. James Hansen and Makiko Sato / csas.earth.Columbia.edu.

The Sea Level Yo-Yo

The sea level changes illustrated in the graph may appear like a yo-yo based on specific events, but are actually natural long-term cycles. These long-term cycles in temperature and sea level are driven primarily by CO_2. Historically, rises in CO_2 came from volcanic activity, decomposition of plants, and releases from the soil and water (only much more recently from the burning of fossil fuels). Over time, the carbon in the atmosphere would decline as it became sequestered—buried again in sediments, captured by plants, and absorbed into water. The historical up and down changes in sea levels meant that corals had to adapt or perish as they typically grow in the first few hundred feet of depth along the coast-line. If sea levels rose a few hundred feet, corals would then be under much deeper water, limiting the amount of sunlight they require to live. Conversely, if sea levels decreased, corals could find themselves living too close to the surface or out of the water unable to survive.

Notice when the historic levels of atmospheric CO_2 rose, they did so quickly, looking like an almost instantaneous rise on the thousand-year scale. Sea levels also rose sharply, sometimes as much as 100 meters (328 feet), indicating that the melting of the ice was relatively quick. When CO_2 levels dropped, they did so gradually over time, indicating the Earth was cooling. Likewise, the drop in sea levels took much longer to occur because the glacier-forming process in the poles is much slower than the glacier-melting process. Is this all sounding a bit familiar to Earth's present state?

Currently, we have a boom in CO_2 emissions and, knowing that global temperatures and sea levels lag this indicator a bit, we know that warming temperatures and rising sea levels will follow as the three lines proceed to maintain their long-term synchronization. There also appear to be upper and lower boundaries for CO_2, global temperature, and sea level: CO_2 ranges between 180–280 parts per million (ppm), the average global temperature rises and falls approximately 5°C (9°F), and sea levels cycle up or down by approximately 120 meters (393 feet).[2]

With these bounds in mind, go back and check out the graph again. At the Earth's previous high CO_2 mark of 280 ppm around 122,000 years ago, sea levels were 25 feet higher than where they are today. As the Earth zooms past the 280-ppm mark to over 400 ppm in 2020, it's scary to imagine what could happen to the (lagging) sea levels in the not-too-distant future.[3]

In historic times with rising CO_2 levels, corals were quickly covered by a dozen or more feet of water in the blink of an eye, geologically speaking. There are places in the Virgin Islands that help illustrate this. In the Virgin Islands there are volcanic islands that have stepwise terraces embedded in the landscape around them—remains of ancient coral reefs. As the volcanoes that made the islands rose over time, they exposed what was happening to the reefs that once fringed their shores. These many terraced steps show that sea level rise was not a single historic event but multiple occurrences that required corals to recolonize to a new depth to live.

On these islands there is undeniable evidence of where the sea levels were in the past and how abruptly they changed over time. If sea levels rose or fell very slowly, then these rocky remains would have created a gradual slope, like a sloped beach. However, that is not the case here as we see numerous and distinctive stepwise terraces left behind that are 10–15 feet (3–4 meters) high. These levels are historical evidence that sea levels, relative to land, changed by a large amount very quickly.

What could produce such a fast change? A rapid rise in sea levels could be caused by an extreme event like a large ice sheet in Greenland slumping into the sea or the carving-off of large deposits of ice from continents or glaciers. Of concern today is the rapid rise in atmospheric CO_2 due to the burning of fossil fuels. Geologic history has demonstrated that sea level rise happens quickly and correlates with high levels of atmospheric CO_2. The fossilized remains of coral reefs are telling us of the past—sea level change can happen quickly—and we should be listening.

9

Coral Sex and Bundles of Joy

A H SEX! The natural imperative to reproduce and advance one's genetic material into the future. All plants and animals have sex in one form or another, and all it takes is for a sperm and egg to meet to create genetically diverse offspring. Sounds easy, right? Not always, as it is not always easy for the egg and sperm to come together in the first place. Sometimes they need outside assistance. The guy at the bar may need a "wing man," flowers need bees for pollination, and our friend the coral often needs help from Mother Ocean and her currents. But yes, corals do have sex! Who knew?

Well, no one knew that until the mid-1980s when Peter Harrison, a leading member of the coral research team at James Cook University, discovered the mass coral spawning phenomenon on the Great Barrier Reef.[1] Through the ages, we learned about the "birds and the bees" by observing sexual encounters in nature. What happened under the sea and how creatures there reproduced, however, was essentially a mystery. If coral polyps had evolved to crawl out of the water and reproduce like the horseshoe crab, or even some fish species that spawn on beach sand, their sex life may have been understood a long time ago.

This was not the case, however. The secret sex lives of corals were not observed until nighttime scuba diving became more popular with the advent of underwater dive lights. We now know corals reproduce sexually using two different methods depending on the species.

Broadcast Spawners

The first type of coral sexual reproduction creates a mass spawning event. These *broadcast spawners* comprise approximately 80% of all scleractinian (hard) corals.[2] Mass spawning events occur once a year on the reef, in the summer just after a full moon, at night, and the entire thing takes about ten to twenty minutes. Consequently, the first divers had to be lucky enough to be in the right place and at just the right time to witness this amazing occurrence.

Coral reefs tend to be very peaceful at night with little activity compared to daylight hours. Most of the reef creatures are typically at rest, making it easier for divers to see them using their lights. So, the divers who witnessed the first spawning events probably paused when they saw fish strangely rise from beneath the sheltered coral outcroppings where they were dozing. They most likely saw crabs, starfish, and other invertebrates crawling out of their sandy burrows, and sea worms rising from crevices within the coral. These first divers to experience this reproductive extravaganza probably had no idea what was happening, but they were witnesses to one of the most beautiful spectacles on earth, under the sea and in the dark.

The other reef creatures unexpectedly become frenzied in the minutes prior to the big event. The corals, in a synchronized pattern, start to release their eggs and sperm in packages known as *gamete bundles* that float upwards to the surface of the ocean (see Images 9.1 and 9.2). Soon the water is full of small spherical white and pink gamete bundles making it hard to see through. After about ten to twenty minutes, the water clears as the spawning has stopped and

Image 9.1

Coral from the genus Acropora releasing their gamete bundles during a spawning event. This genus tends to have pink gamete bundles.

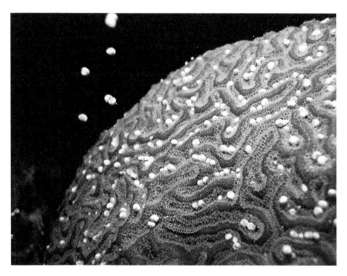

Image 9.2

During a spawning event, gamete bundles from the symmetrical brain coral (Pseudodiploria strigosa) are released into grooves and then make their way up to the surface.
Photo credit: Emma Hickerson/NOAA/FGBNMS.

all of these gamete bundles are now at the surface. There can be several bundles of eggs released from a coral polyp, or several bundles of sperm, or even several bundles of eggs and sperm packaged together. There are male and female coral polyps, as well as polyps that are both male and female or hermaphroditic. The release of the gamete bundles is the first step in the dance of coral sex, but let's back up and see how this process develops.

Gametogenesis—How It All Begins

Generally, preparation for the spawning event starts many months ahead of time. The corals sense the number of daylight hours increasing in tandem with the waters getting warmer as summer approaches. Corals can sense even the smallest change in temperature and light as they use the sunlight for a good portion of their energy. These subtle environmental changes over many weeks also cause specific changes in their polyp physiology. They start to get into "condition" for the spawning event to occur.

The getting-ready process for the spawning event is scientifically called *gametogenesis* and is where previously stored fats (lipids) are used to create the gamete bundles. As gametogenesis proceeds and the time of release (spawning) nears, the look of each coral polyp changes in a process called *setting-up*. Remember, in a polyp there is only one way in and one way out—through the mouth. So, in addition to the ingestion of food and the release of waste, this is also where the spawn release action happens (see Image 9.3). (The coral mouth is an amazingly versatile opening!)

This setting-up behavior makes each polyp look different as they start the outward extension of themselves for these bundles to be released. One can actually see the inflated size of the polyps, the extension of the mouth opening, followed by the appearance of the gamete bundle starting to make its journey out of the opening. This is not unlike what we call

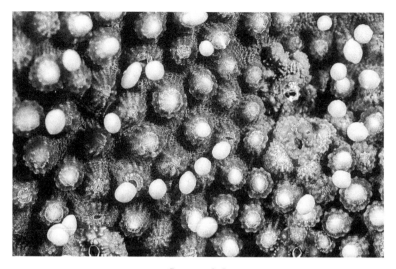

Image 9.3
Polyps of boulder star coral (Orbicella franksi) releasing gamete bundles through its mouth. Photo credit: G.P. Schmahl, NOAA, FGBNMS.

crowning when a human baby's head starts to appear from the birth canal.

As the magical spawning moment gets closer, the small fish on the reef start to get excited, anticipating a good meal of gamete bundles. Likewise, the larger fish in turn start anticipating a good meal of the smaller fish. Invertebrates perk up and get into the action as well. Polychaetae worms, brittle starfish, and shrimp-like amphipods all sense something different is about to happen. Whether they are as good with their own natural calendar or biological clock, or whether there is some discernable smell or taste in the water, scientists are not sure.

And then it begins rather quickly. One gamete bundle after the other emerges from the polyp. Polyps, in general, will each release approximately 3–12 consecutive bulbous gamete bundles in this fashion. The bundles are either pink or white, depending on the species, and soon it starts to look like an upside-down snowstorm on the reef (see Image 9.4).

Image 9.4
Coral spawning in the Flower Garden Banks National
Marine Sanctuary in the northwestern Gulf of Mexico.
Spawning reefs everywhere will look like an upside-down
snowstorm for several minutes while the gametes float to the surface.
Photo credit: Emma Hickerson/NOAA/FGBNMS.

This is an entire reef event, and some reefs can stretch for miles. It is a remarkable act of coordination almost as if there was a conductor directing the show across the entire reef. How this is accomplished by a colony of single polyps that do not have a coordinated nervous system driven by a centralized brain remains a mystery. Somehow, each coral polyp on an entire reef that is comprised of different coral colonies knows the exact moment to release its bundle.

Of course, this spawning process is not without challenges. Along the bottom, all the fish, prawns, worms, and other creatures swim in a frenzied celebration of this yearly feast. They sense the impending release of these gamete bundles, which, due to their high lipid and protein content, make an excellent and nutritious meal. Consequently, many of the gamete bundles are eaten before they ever reach the surface (see Image 9.5).

Image 9.5
This brittle star is out in full force having a feast during the spawning snowstorm. Photo credit: Emma Hickerson, NOAA, FGBNMS.

Sex on the Ocean's Surface

In moments, surviving coral gamete bundles with eggs or sperm, or both, slowly rise and reach the surface of the water. They are then ruptured by wave action and surface air. Like a balloon bursting when it hits a sharp object, the gamete bundles break apart, casting millions upon millions of eggs and billions of sperm onto the water surface. And here is where they will stay for days or weeks. Their stored lipids serve both as their energy source and life preserver for their new journey on the surface, subject to the whims of current and wind. This floating layer of sperm, eggs, and developing larvae is called a coral *spawning slick* and sometimes can be seen from the air.

Once the eggs and sperm have been released from their gamete bundles, they hope to encounter fertilization partners from corals of the same species, but from different genetic strains. Finding a competent sperm for an egg, or an egg for a sperm, somewhere in the watery surface currents, is the goal.

Timing is critical. The sperm must find an appropriate egg to fertilize within the first few hours or else it will die. They don't have the luxury of courtship. Even though they survived the journey to the surface, they still must rely on the waves and currents to bring the released eggs and sperm into contact for a perfect match. Once fertilization takes place, the larval stage will develop in about 24 hours. The biological sequence from the gamete bundles of joy to swimming baby coral larvae all happen at the surface of the ocean.

Around the world this takes place in the heat of the summer season, which is also the peak of hurricane and monsoon season. The odds of survival from the larval stage to an adult coral colony are a mere 1 in a million over the course of a hundred years. How would you like those odds? One in a million, every century, if the conditions are right.

The Brooders

The second type of coral sexual reproduction, by *brooders*, is quite different than those of broadcast spawners. Brooders keep their eggs inside of the polyp where they are fertilized by sperm of a nearby, genetically unrelated, strain of the same species. They hold their developing young inside for a short period of time. This protects the gametes during the critical fertilization stage and allows for the fertilized egg to develop into a swimming larva in about 24 hours, at which point they are released from the parent polyp. Because this happens inside the polyp of brooding corals, not much is known about their embryonic development into swimming larvae.

Brooders' embryonic development may be similar to that of broadcast spawners, which we can observe. We know once the egg is fertilized the first cell division happens within the first hour. The roundish zygote turns from looking like the original egg into what looks more like a double-yoke chicken egg in the frying pan. Then each of those two new cells divide again making four. They divide again into eight, then again into 16. Their division continues until there are many thousands of cells that start to look like a large bunch of grapes. However, they are no larger than the original egg at this time—only thousands of smaller cells specializing in function as the larvae develop.

For brooders and broadcast spawners, it takes about 24 hours to go from the fertilized egg stage to the larval free-swimming stage. For both, they have all the specialized cells needed to move, swim, tell direction, and engage in typical larval behaviors. This is the first independent stage of a coral's life.

We call it swimming but, in reality, it is moving in a direction at the mercy of the currents and waves. Brooders may spawn a few times a year and during those 3–4 days, a few spawns will take place, normally near the new moon instead of the full moon like the broadcast spawners. The new moon means darkness underwater so the more fully developed larvae will remain hidden from the predators as they look for a place to settle. Amazingly, the larvae released from the brooder parent already have the algal and microbial partners (symbionts) given to them by their parents.

Spit for Spat

We see broadcast spawners and brooders in some oyster species as well. American oysters are broadcast spawners and release sperm or eggs into the water near the same time to optimize the chances of millions of eggs becoming fertilized. The Chilean oyster and the European flat oyster are brooders. They also brood their young oyster larvae inside the parent shell space and then spit out the tiny larval shelled juveniles as *spat*. Therefore, the offspring of these shellfish are also called spat. This is also the real reason why people used to not eat oysters in months not having an "R" in them. It was not because of the summer heat but because the shelled larvae were being brooded inside of those oysters and eating them was like chewing sand. This *spit-for-spat* strategy seems to also work well for brooding corals. By just spitting out a few new baby corals right in the neighborhood, but not expanding much beyond the home site, survival rates are better.

Whether accomplished by simultaneously spawning eggs and sperm from an entire reef or releasing fully formed larvae from brooding parents, corals have fascinating strategies for their sexual reproduction as we will see in the next chapter.

10

A Deep Dive into Sexual Strategies

WHAT IS the best way to keep your species growing in population and advancing across generations? Corals have been working on the answer. The environment in which they live, and the fact that they are stationary creatures, has made this a challenging endeavor. Some coral species are quite interesting in that they produce both eggs and sperm in one colony, while others produce only one or the other. Importantly, this means they cannot fertilize themselves. Successful fertilization requires eggs and sperm from corals of the same species, but from genetically different strains. Because potential fertilization partners may be miles away, and their gametes are at the mercy of ocean currents, actual fertilization can be rare. So, the answer for corals has been to develop two evolutionary strategies to enhance their odds of successful fertilization.

In the previous chapter two different types of sexual reproduction were discussed. Corals that produced the upside-down snowstorm are called *broadcast spawners*. With great synchronization among corals on the reef, they cast their gamete bundles into the ocean currents and they are done.

The other type exhibited by corals is known as *brooding*, where the coral polyps take additional care of their fertilized eggs by holding them internally for a period of time, resulting in the spawning of fewer, but more developed, larvae.

Broadcast spawning and brooding are types of *reproductive strategies*. We see these two different strategies for reproduction in many kinds of plants and animals in nature. The first strategy sows many potential offspring without providing any further help, and the other sows a lower number of offspring but with added protection and longer-term care from the parent. Scientists call these *r* and *K* strategies, respectively.

The r-strategy bets on sheer numbers, producing and releasing a huge amount of offspring and then letting them fend for themselves. The K-strategy group is more like some of the higher plants and animals—they take care of a fewer number of offspring for a longer time before letting them go to fend for themselves. In this strategy smaller numbers of offspring are produced, but hopefully with an increased chance for survival.

r-Strategy

Broadcast spawners (the r-group) generate a larger number of eggs (sometimes millions), or sperm (by the billions), in hopes of producing at least one surviving offspring. There is no touching, emotion, or parental care involved here, just the phenomenal, synchronized release of gamete bundles. Everything else happens outside of the colony on the surface of the ocean and beyond.

The journey for larvae from broadcast spawners is a totally *non-feeding* event, which means it is only fueled by the stored lipids (fat) nutritional reserve from the parent egg. As a microscopic creature, it does not carry a lot of rations. The amount of time before it can feed itself—or have the algal partners contribute to the kitchen table—could be weeks or months. This is what the broadcast spawners must deal with, but because of sheer numbers and the increased distribution distances across new colonies, this has been a successful strategy in the recent past.

In the ocean, where currents and waves can disperse the next generation, you will find fish that are pelagic spawners with the same strategy as the broadcast spawning corals. Some of these fish may live on coral reefs or nearshore environments for the majority of their lives, but they move to the open water (pelagic zone) of the ocean to spawn. Millions of eggs and sperm from marine fish are released and the rest of the story is downstream. Fish like grouper, snapper, and others may up their odds by moving to an aggregation location where many individuals of the same species seasonally migrate in order to release their gametes at the same time and location. This improves the odds of fertilization and the chance that some will reach adulthood even if there are plenty of predators waiting to devour a large portion of these nutritional eggs.

For broadcast spawners, the r-strategy is quite a dynamic evolutionary strategy compared to what we'll soon learn of their brooding counterparts. Time will tell us in the near future which is the more effective way to procreate and survive in light of all the environmental challenges that are increasingly affecting our oceans.

K-Strategy

The eggs of brooding corals (the K-group) are fertilized within the polyp. For them, this means taking in a small amount of sperm spawned from a different colony nearby and letting the sperm fertilize the internally held eggs. The chances of the eggs being fertilized successfully are very good, but the number of growing fertilized eggs that can be held inside the coral polyp are limited due to the increase in size of the fertilized eggs as they develop into larvae. The number of brooding larvae released are in the thousands, not millions.

The distance the brooded larvae swim away from its parent polyp is much shorter than the free ride taken by the broadcast spawned larvae on the surface of the ocean. The evolutionary strategy of the brooders is quite different from that of the broadcast spawners.

K-strategy marine fish are called demersal spawners and they release their gametes on, or near, the sea bed (demersal zone). The parents of these species provide more protective care for at least part of the time during the development of their young into larvae. The anemone fish, or clown fish, described earlier in the symbiotic relationship with the anemone, is one such example of a demersal spawning species. The larger female lays eggs in a nest of sorts attached to a hard, rock-like surface. Each egg is attached to the prior cleaned area of a bare rock on the reef that may be 1–6 inches in diameter. The smaller male diligently fertilizes those eggs as they are laid or attached. The male then guards the nest from both predators and other clownfish as the eggs develop, while also helping to keep the nest area clean. He performs these tasks diligently and continuously, from a few days to over a week, ensuring the survival of his offspring.

r- vs. K-Strategies in the Future

Before human-induced climate change, there might not have been significant differences in the survival rates of coral larvae produced by brooders and broadcast spawners. How those numbers are changing as our planet moves forward is certainly an area for future research. What we do know now is that there are significant differences in the distance the larval offspring produced by each strategy can travel and this can affect overall survivability. If it is possible to expand their territory, to send their offspring farther away, it may allow colonization in an area that may have better conditions for survival. However, the reverse is also possible and seems more likely; if offspring are carried far away from the conditions that allowed the parent to be successful enough to survive, grow, and reproduce, the parental home environment may have been a better fit.

An example of this is seen in mustard hill corals. They are brooders and appear to currently have a considerable reproductive advantage over their broadcast spawning coral counterparts by producing larger offspring, closer to home. The reason for this is simple: the oceanic environment has not been this hostile to corals since the last major extinction event 65 million years ago. Even in the best of conditions, without major hurricanes, without high ocean acidity, and without rising water temperatures, it's incredibly rare for broadcast spawners to survive—only about one in a million broadcast spawned larvae actually survive to become an adult colony.[1] Presently, it's even harder as more corals are dying from disease or bleaching events, causing the distance between reproductively viable broadcaster corals to grow even further apart.

This increase in the distance between broadcast spawners lowers the chances of fertilization, the first required hurdle for reproductive success. This is called the *Alee Effect* and was based on the writings of W.C. Alee, who was one of the great pioneers of American ecology (1885–1955). Over 70 years ago, he was concerned by dwindling population sizes of many species and the impact on future conservation efforts. Clearly, those concerns are still valid today. If populations of reproducing organisms become too scarce, it is increasingly more difficult for fertilization among sexually reproductive organisms to take place. For example, when songbirds become so rare that they cannot hear the song of a potential mate, it is difficult to have a courtship. Likewise, if broadcast spawners become fewer and farther apart, it is hard to ensure future fertilization can be successful. On the flip side, the brooders spawn their larvae closer to where they live. Once settled and grown, their chance of successful fertilization from nearby colonies is much greater.

Saving the Unicorn

One impressive looking broadcast spawner is the pillar coral. It can grow very tall and resemble a cluster of cigars, or slender tree stumps, growing up from the sea floor. This is a favorite among divers, one they like to pose in front of for photos. However, this coral is now in a critical status of being "reproductively extinct." While there are still a few of these majestic corals in existence, they are very far apart from each other. Therefore, the chances of the sperm from one contacting the eggs from another are increasingly difficult. Even though they still produce gametes and release them in synchrony, the possibilities of fertilization taking place between the gametes of two different strains of pillar corals is growing dim. It's like an SOS signal that is sent but never received, floating away into oblivion. A conservation effort has taken place to save and repopulate these corals in Florida and the Caribbean named "Saving the Unicorn" after the hornlike shape on the mythical creature. For this project, gametes were collected from the few colonies now separated by miles of ocean and successfully fertilized in the laboratory in order to make more. In addition, plans to outplant future colonies in close approximation to each other will increase the odds that future fertilization will take place.[2]

Fragments of Hope

In another effort to get broadcast spawners closer to each other, scientists are working on a project in Belize called "Fragments of Hope." They are taking fragments from colonies of the same pillar coral, successfully grown in field nurseries, and outplanting them near genetically different colonies. This is an easy way to increase the odds that eggs and sperm from different genotypes will be close enough for fertilization to occur during a spawning event. Proximity matters, particularly with dwindling populations that become isolated enough to decrease the chances of sexual reproduction, as the Alee Effect has demonstrated. This simple intervention of outplanting potential breeding colonies closer together may become a relatively easy way to increase the odds that fertilization takes place among the broadcast spawners. Simply put, let's keep coral sex closer to home.

11

The Fantastic Journey and Search for the First and Final Home

L IKE ANY other r-species (those that produce many off-spring with only a few getting to adulthood), coral sexual reproduction strategies by broadcast spawners usually start with millions of eggs and then drop daily from there. Sometimes called *the gauntlet of death*, it is the typical growth curve for many marine invertebrates where millions of larvae are reduced to a very small group of extremely lucky survivors.

The Coral Slick

After the egg is fertilized, it quickly develops into a moving and spinning microscopic-sized larval form within the first 24 hours. The tiny larvae look like small ovals or round globs with hair-like structures called *cilia*. The cilia act like oars, helping to steer the larvae. For coral larvae, there is no apparent head or tail, or any sensory structure that we can see, which makes their amazing ocean journey all the more fascinating. Coral larvae can mix in with plankton and be carried by currents for hundreds of miles, making very little headway against it. However, later in development, the larvae can make relatively small positional and directional changes while being taken on this ocean ride. In large numbers they have been known to form a slick on the ocean surface, and some can be seen for miles (Image 11.1).

While being stuck in this slick, their movement is determined by the wind and current. The combination of constant directional winds and similar wave action may accumulate the larvae into floating rows similar to seafoam. When the larvae are aggregated this way on the ocean surface, they are mostly orange, bronze, and light red in color. This makes them easily identifiable from the various algal blooms such as a red tide, which is a dark red. In

Image 11.1

Just after spawning, coral gametes float to the surface of the ocean and form a coral slick. This photo was taken at night in the Flower Garden Banks National Marine Sanctuary in the Gulf of Mexico. Coral slicks look light orange and red during daylight hours. Photo credit: NOAA.

some confined bodies of water, the shifting winds between shorelines can cause the larvae to move back and forth on the water surface, creating a very odd color. One theory is that the Red Sea received its name from such an event, although algal red tides, the sunsets which typically reflect light from the red sands of the mountain shoreline, and any combination of these are also likely sources.

Since the larvae are literally stuck to the surface of the ocean for what could be either days or weeks—depending on the species—they are quite vulnerable to predation. As with any food source in the ocean, there are always predators, large and small, ready to devour members of the slick. Even larger plankton-eating organisms such as whale sharks and manta rays are drawn to them like microscopic candies. Some seem to time their feeding migrations to coincide with the spawning events of coral and other organisms to take advantage of the nutritious meals they provide.

For surviving coral larvae, currents and storms can help them along the way to their ultimate reef destination. They may also hinder survival by either carrying them farther away from reefs or forcing them up onto the shoreline, resulting in additions to the always growing group of the many who never cross the larval settlement finish line.

The Descent

The next part of this fantastic journey becomes even more exciting as the larvae begin to slowly sink. During their time as planktonic larvae they metabolize stored lipids (fats) as food—the same lipids that kept them afloat on the surface. When enough of the lipids have been consumed the larvae can pull themselves away from the surface tension of the ocean and start their search for the perfect home. It's like having an inflatable life vest, or buoyancy compensator, that has released enough air to allow the swimmer to slowly make their way into the lower depths. This descent is not direct, but more like a slow-motion expedition.

Remember the description of the spawning event with gamete bundles floating upward to the surface? Well, the cycle is now completed as the developing larvae who have survived the journey so far make their way back down to the ocean floor. The larvae are no longer moving according to the whims of wind, waves, and current. At this point they have a small yet meaningful way to control where they go.

The Search for Home

Still mostly invisible to the naked eye, the larvae start their journey to the benthic, or bottom dwelling, phase of life. What's truly amazing is that the larvae don't just randomly hope to land in a suitable environment. They don't want a sand bottom, mud bottom, or seagrass meadow, but something that more resembles their place of origin. Somehow, they can *sense* existing reefs and then swim towards them. We have no idea how they do this as the larvae have no eyes, ears, nose, mouth—or any other sensory organ we can identify. But they do indeed have the ability to sense many things as determined by experimental flume tests performed in laboratories. In general terms, these tests place coral larvae in a tank that has two different sources of water leading into it. One source of water contains a variable to test, and the other does not. As the tank fills, the larvae have a choice of which direction to swim. If they like the variable that is introduced, the larvae will gather in the location of that water source.

From these tests it was determined that coral larvae can respond to taste (or is it smell?), and even detect light and colors.[1] Given the choice of swimming towards or away from the direction of water from a healthy reef, they always choose to move towards the healthier source. There is no advantage to swimming towards a mud bottom, a bare sand area, or even a sea grass meadow. Furthermore, settlement studies have shown that coral larvae have the ability to determine the location of orange, red, and pink colors.[2] These are the colors of crustose coralline algae, a preferable surface location with which to attach. When these algae are ground up into powder and placed in a flume, coral larvae will demonstrate searching behavior and accelerate towards it.

What's even more remarkable is that similar tests have shown that larvae use sound in addition to smell to find existing reefs.[3] Most people find this surprising, and indeed, legendary adventurer Jacques Cousteau himself may be in part to blame for once calling the ocean the "Silent World." However, in reality, underwater life is anything but silent. The large number of invertebrates such as snapping shrimp, rapidly closing bivalves, barnacles, and more, emit a crackling type of sound depicting a thriving reef. But hmmm . . . where are the ears on these round ciliated larvae? How do they hear anything at all? The short answer is that we don't know, but they seem to be able to utilize a multitude of senses in their search for the best place to land.

The Landing

Once the larvae land, they do not immediately put down roots on the first piece of real estate they encounter. Usually, they *test* the new locale first, possibly for factors that will affect its life directly like temperature, pH, available space for growth, etc. They bounce around until they find the best possible spot. It's vital they get this right—once a larva attaches itself to a spot on the ground, there's no changing its mind (as if we can actually think of a larva having a mind to change).

The actual landing onto a permanent home space for a coral can best be described as a hot air balloon trying to land on uneven terrain. In fact, that is what it looks like under a microscope. Picture a balloon-shaped larva, barely able to make headway upstream and hoping for a landing site downstream, bouncing around the ocean floor and frequently touching down. If the environment isn't deemed suitable upon first contact, there's no settlement and the larva is bouncing off to the next potential location. When all the right conditions are present and the coral larva finds what it believes to be just the right spot, it appears to "sit down" to literally stick the landing. Houston, the coral larva has safely landed!

The journey for brooding corals is a much shorter one, as once the fertilized egg becomes larva it is released from the polyp of the female colony and searches for a substrate usually close by. When it finds just the right spot, it too takes a sit-down position. For both the spawned and brooded larvae, they are now at a critical juncture of their respective journeys, and despite the different pathways each took to find their place, the road ahead will now be the same for both. To begin, each will undergo a metamorphosis that is critical to the settlement process—attaching to the substrate, which can be any hard rock-like substance on the ocean floor. This attachment process is also known as *recruitment*. Once the free-swimming larva attaches to the substrate, it can transform into a polyp.

Even though it took a series of fortunate events to get this far, the survival rate from here on out is still very low. Our new coral has been recruited to the substrate, but the polyp is still no bigger than the pinhead-sized larva that produced it. Although it is quite small, it is a polyp, aptly called the *primary polyp* (Image 11.2). It can remain this size for weeks, months, or even a year before growing up to become an adult-sized polyp. How fast the primary polyp will grow into an adult depends on the species of coral, available nutrition, and environmental conditions.

During this time, it has to survive the onslaught of native benthic reef-cleaning grazers that scour the bottom to eat the algae and any other living organism they come across. Most grazers, such as snails and sea urchins, are oblivious to

Image 11.2
A magnified image of a primary polyp of an elkhorn coral.
It can take a few weeks for the settled larva to reach this stage
of development. This polyp is about the size of the tip of a pen.
Photo credit: Dan Mele.

what else is growing in their path. As an innocent bystander in a pasture of grazers, the coral polyp can become collateral damage. It may not have been the target of anyone's food line march, but it can be consumed or destroyed in the process. In a benthic arena there are always threats to coral, regardless of their size. The large 100-year-old boulder corals, the small 3–5-year-old branching corals, and the microscopic new developing corals all face threats of one form or another.

All of them are legitimately corals, but only the coral colonies bigger than about 3 cm, or the size of a golf ball, are counted as "a coral" in scientific survey monitoring. Not just because this size is big enough to be easily observed by a diver, but also because corals less than this size may not survive. So, in addition to being in the path of diverse biological grazing machines, the coral must now start feeding on its own.

Feeding

Brooding corals are not as susceptible to starvation once they recruit onto the substrate because they already have the algal partners supplied by their parents. The larvae from broadcast spawners have had the challenge of operating as non-feeding larvae and now have to somehow acquire their algal partners once they land. So, how does a newly settled coral from broadcast spawners get the algae it needs to start its own algal farm inside its living tissue? Unfortunately, it is not clearly understood how this starts but we do know that it takes time, sometimes quite a while. It is amazing how a small coral polyp can survive so long without its main food source, and researchers hope one day to figure out how they do it.

We do know that when the algae *infect* (or inoculate) the coral tissue, the developing coral also starts the growth process to enlarge in size from the small primary polyp to the larger adult-sized polyp. The adult polyp will soon reproduce asexually. From here on out, it is "divide and conquer"—one polyp divides into two, two will become four, etc. As months go by, you will have a few dozen polyps which by the end of year one will become approximately the size of a pencil eraser (Image 11.3). This growth is faster in some, and slower in others, but eventually will result in a clearly visible growing colony. It will take between 10–20 years for a primary elkhorn polyp (Image 11.2) to grow into a colony large enough to sexually reproduce (Image 11.4).

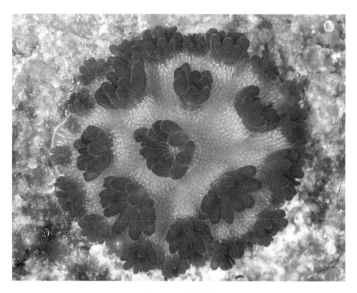

Image 11.3

A magnification of the colony formed from the primary polyp of elkhorn coral. It is approximately two months old and just under a centimeter in diameter. This small colony was created through asexual reproduction and each little polyp is genetically identical. Photo credit: Dan Mele.

Image 11.4

A mature and majestic elkhorn coral colony.

Man-Made Impediments

Remember that during spawning events very few eggs are fertilized and become larvae. What is even more amazing is that only about one larva out of every million makes it to an adult colony,[4] in a reproductive process that only occurs every 10, 50, or 100 years—depending on the species and environmental conditions. If you live to be 800 years old and are only successful in reproducing once every century or so, it works. In today's world, however, that historical survival percentage may be terribly skewed as there are other factors that can kill the larvae disproportionately on their journey or kill the developing polyp when it is attached. Unfortunately, one of these man-made impediments is the all-too-common oil spill.

Oil spills can greatly affect coral larvae as they travel along the ocean surface. Oil and coral larvae both float on the surface of the ocean in films. The stored lipids in the coral larvae place them in the same buoyant position as oil. When coral larvae get caught up in an oil spill of any size, it is certain death for them. With modern oil explorations, and potential transport spillage, there is a continued threat to coral larvae. In addition, recent oil spill remediation practices have used dispersants to make oil slicks disappear out of sight. Oil dispersants form globules around the oil, allowing it to sink.[5] While this helps with the public perception that the problem is gone, all this really does is sink the oil to the waters below, meaning potential disaster for existing coral and devastation for future coral if this happens during spawning season.

12

Coral Wars—Slow Motion Fighting with Specialized Weapons

SURPRISINGLY, CORALS have amazing weaponry to ensure they can defend and feed themselves. Each polyp also has the ability to grow weapons for war and they have weapons of mass destruction that reside internally. This is extremely important for a creature who is attached to the ocean floor and cannot flee its enemies. It is also helpful for coral to gain critical territory as it grows. Coral polyps can defend themselves individually, but they also will coordinate with each other when portions of the colony fight in wars to benefit the colony as a whole. They are good soldiers when they have to be.

An Outer Armor of Defense

The first line of defense for the coral polyp occurs in a mucous layer that envelops them externally in every nook and cranny. A fabulous protective barrier, it also contains a microbiome which has a large percentage of bacteria that defend the coral against disease from other invading bacteria, viruses, and fungal agents. This microbial army is always at work, keeping the mucous layer—or outer armor—free from enemy troops. If any invading pathogens gain a foothold within this layer, disease and death could spread throughout the coral colony.

Interestingly, when coral is broken it will quickly form even more mucous. Perhaps this excess production is to enable faster transfer of the microbes to the place of injury. If coral is taken out of the water or exposed to air from an extremely low tide on a shallow reef, excess mucous may be produced to keep the coral from drying out. During my first expedition to the Virgin Islands at the age of 13, I noticed that coral samples I collected produced a lot of mucous and had a very distinctive smell. I encountered the smell again decades later by deliberately cutting corals for restoration work. Future research will help us to understand if this odor is somehow related to the defense of the coral.

Tentacles Armed with Stinging Cells

The tentacles of a polyp that surround their mouth are used for hunting prey and for defense. They have stinging cells (nematocysts) located in the tentacles. These stinging cells look like miniature whaling harpoons—loaded, locked, and ready for action. Essentially, they are preloaded weapons with curled-up barbs and triggering mechanisms, which fire off on their own by physical stimulation (Image 12.1). This may sound "barbaric," but it is one of the main characteristics that make up this special phylum to which corals belong (Cnidarian).

Several corals' close relatives—jellyfish and sea anemones—have this stinging capability as well. Many of us have personally experienced the unpleasant stinging sensation in the ocean either from direct contact with a jellyfish or by encountering stinging cells in the water that have separated from jellyfish through wave action at the beach.

Image 12.1

These are the polyps of the great star coral (Montastraea cavernosa). Look closely and you can see regular tentacles sticking out of most of the polyps. The polyps on the right must feel threatened in some way because they have extended their sweeping tentacles and are ready for battle. Photo credit: Dan Mele.

Sea anemones, which can look like very large individual coral polyps, are stalked creatures with many tentacles that surround a centralized mouth. Within the tentacles and mouth area are microscopic stinging cells similar to the coral polyp. These stinging cells do not fire when the tentacles touch each other because the anemone recognizes itself. If a fish or any other type of prey comes within reach of the tentacles, the stinging cells are triggered, and the anemone uses its tentacles to bring the repeatedly stung prey into its mouth. The only fish that can evade this fate is the clownfish, the constant companion of the sea anemone.

While coral polyps get much of their nutrition from their zooxanthellae partners, they also feed themselves by pulling prey from the sea, similar to the anemone but on a much smaller scale. Coral polyps have fewer tentacles then an anemone, typically six (or multiples of six) for hard corals or eight tentacles per polyp for soft corals. At night, coral polyps will extend their bodies up and partially out of their corallite homes. While they are extended, they filter out food from the water passing through. When a small bit of food, such as a piece of fish or a small zooplankton, passes by, the coral polyp will zap it with its stinging cells. Once the morsel is secured by the stinging cells, the polyp uses its tentacles to move it slowly towards its mouth. Just as a fish is caught by a fisherman, the coral polyp's tentacles hook its dinner with one or more stinging cells, "harpoon" it, and reel it in. "Fish-on" or should I say "plankton-on!"

Coral polyps will also use their stinging cells defensively to ward off any tiny predators. These predators include many various marine invertebrates, such as polychaetes (known as bristle worms), shrimp, and crabs. Many of these creatures may want to take a nibble of them. A coral's only possible response is to sting them repeatedly. Coral polyps in the same colony somehow recognize each other and will not sting each other. Even more amazingly, polyps in a colony will work in unison to fight off a predator.

Sweeping Tentacles

The stinging cell weapons so meticulously used for hunting and defense are also destructive weapons used in coral wars. As corals grow, they expand over the surrounding territory. When corals grow towards each other, a battle for territory takes place. These stinging cells are used as weapons to keep other organisms from growing on top of a coral's own territory, thus preventing them from taking over a portion of the colony. It is akin to a "capture more room and grow or risk being grown over" survival strategy.

This maneuver has been classically documented using time lapse photography with large sea anemones found in intertidal pools. Here, the anemones have the chance to slowly give up, detach themselves, move on, and move away. Because coral polyps are stationary, they often end up in a fight to the death instead.

Before a war starts, polyps near the outer edge of the colony will actually go through a physical transformation. These outer polyps (or advancing troops) still have their standard issue tentacles described above, but they will start to grow longer-sized weaponry.[1] They extend one or two very long *sweeping tentacles*. These extremely elongated tentacles have high concentrations of stinging cells at the tips. The coral uses its sweeping tentacles to determine if any other critter or coral is in its proximity and to be sure no one else is already settled there (see Image 12.2).

If the space is essentially clear, corals start to prepare the grounds by stinging small organisms, such as algae and microbes, to clean and prepare the surface. The coral needs a clean surface for the new lateral extension polyps to adhere to so they can't be dislodged. If you have ever tried to glue something on a dirty surface, you know why this is an important step for the coral.

After the initial sweeping process, the outer-rim polyps split in two to form new outer rim polyps as the colony expands laterally. If there happens to be another type of coral right next door, a war may be on the horizon.

Deadly Battles for Territory

Coral wars take place at night and in very slow motion. They typically last just a few nights before the outcome is established. (Maybe all human wars should be in slow motion and only a last few nights!) When looking at sped-up time lapse photos of the combat, tentacles of warring corals flail around

Image 12.2

These coral polyps have regular tentacles surrounding the mouth of each polyp and some have longer specialized sweeping tentacles. Photo credit: G.P. Schmahl, FGBNMS, NOAA.

like arms of an alien beast. While all corals extend their bodies to increase the reach of their tentacles, some are able to grow their tentacles into menacing weapons of war. Once a war starts, the sweeping tentacles, which look like whips with hooks, thrash around as the advancing polyps from both colonies try to sting each other to death. Eventually either a winner emerges or a truce is established.

If there is no truce, then it is a fight to the death. The winner gains territory. The loser in smaller colonies has all or most of its polyps killed. If a portion of a larger colony avoids the sweeping tentacles and death, it may live—at least for a little while. In time, the winner will grow closer to the loser again, wanting even more territory and another war will break out.

If a truce is established between two warring coral colonies, one of two things can occur. The two colonies can either build up tissue right up to each other, essentially starting vertical growth instead of lateral growth (The Wall) (see Image 12.3). Or they can keep a division or space between them as a truce line or demilitarized zone (The DMZ). Either way, a war was waged and then ended, most times in 1–2 days.

Image 12.3

These are two different colonies of knobby brain coral (Pseudodiploria clivosa). Because they are from different genotypes (not clones) they will battle for space when they encroach upon each other's territory. In this case, they have essentially grown into each other and created a border wall of sorts. Photo credit: Dan Mele.

Afterwards, the corals involved show the ravages of war, from flesh-wound paling to full tissue loss, with polyps killed and missing in action. You can see evidence and outcomes of past coral wars on the ocean floor where many corals live in dense proximity to each other. Two adjacent corals may have left an empty lot between them like a DMZ. Or, they will live right up next to each other, growing a border wall. This signifies that some sort of peace has been reached, one that often will last for centuries.

Another Weapon: One of Mass Destruction

Using highly weaponized sweeper tentacles that make beautiful and intricate shapes as they move through the water before landing on the other polyp or colony is one way corals engage in warfare. However, another type of weapon some corals use is similar to weapons of mass destruction or even chemical warfare. It originates from the inside of the polyps.

To use this weapon, polyps will eject their mesenterial filaments—essentially the guts of the polyp—onto an adversary, complete with digestive juices and, yes, more stinging cells. It is sort of like throwing up on your enemy by slinging strands of your stomach mucous filled with digestive enzymes. This behavior kills polyps within reach of the vomited strands as the digestive juices destroy them from the outside. Afterwards, the polyps retract the mesenterial filaments and perhaps some nutrition as well from the losing polyps (see Image 12.4).

Many home aquarium owners with tanks of dense corals have witnessed the remains of white strands on top of one coral next to another coral and wondered, "What just happened?" For corals in saltwater tanks, as in the wild, if you can't sting them to death, then puke on them and try to digest them, even if they are out of reach of your tentacles. Beautiful coral reefs, so tranquil to look at during the day, are certainly a different place at night.

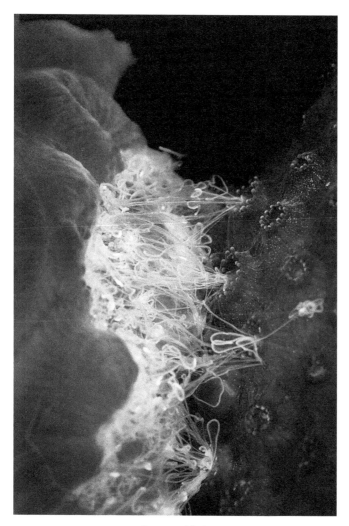

Image 12.4

The boulder star coral (Orbicella annularis) on the right is expelling mesenterial filaments onto the great star coral (Montastraea cavernosa) on the left. Look closely at the boulder star coral and you can see the mesenterial filaments coming out of the mouths of some of the polyps. These filaments contain digestive acids and stinging cells, and those polyps on the receiving end will become severely injured or killed. For coral warfare, these are indeed weapons of mass destruction.
Photo credit: Dan Mele.

Like coral spawning, it is very easy to miss a coral war since they are mostly fought at night when normal full polyp extension takes place. During the day, corals seem to have a truce, a cease fire perhaps, or a time to rest and rethink war strategy—all while they are retracted and resting in their calcium carbonate cup. I can just imagine them thinking: "Hey, what happened to Charlie? His polyp was just here yesterday."

On a natural reef, corals of the same species typically have different genotypes (the primary polyp created from different parents). On occasion, coral heads can break, and pieces will get distributed here and there on the reef to form new colonies. If these related colonies (clones) eventually meet up and send out sweeper tentacles, they will recognize each other as being genetically the same—"one of their own." There is no resulting war or "death by friendly fire." How they instantly recognize polyps of their own colony is unclear, but this behavior is very important for restoration efforts, as discussed in future chapters.

The Aftermath of War

During the day, the results of territory wars are more apparent to the trained eye. In a dense reef with high coral cover, the growth patterns and territory boundaries can be better understood by observing which individual is now growing over the top of another. Just like the growth of trees in a forest, they grow up towards the sunlight that gives them their main energy and capitalize on as much of that as possible. As trees all struggle for the sunlight in a mature canopy forest, corals are doing the same thing, just much more slowly.

Even though these coral wars sound a bit gruesome, ultimately, they make for a beautiful reef. The upward expansion of new coral branches and the lateral extension of massive coral growing into boulder size heads (or *bombies* as they are called down under on the Great Barrier Reef), all have a history of war. They are the result of high competition for space and light by many different coral species.

The diversity of coral species, structural formations, and space utilization on a reef are all very important to life on earth. Nearly all undersea organisms use the three-dimensional space, holes, and crevasses that corals create for their habitat and protection. Also, the upward formation of reef structures as they reach for sunlight gives all creatures—under the sea and on land—protection from storm surge and shoreline erosion.

13

Cosmic Inner Space and Deepwater Corals

WHAT IS the difference between an "innie" and an "outie?" No, I am not talking about belly buttons, but instead reference points relative to where we live in the cosmos. Outer space and inner space are vastly different from each other, and from our normal existence on Earth. Standing on land we should take the time to contemplate the outer world above us as well as the inner world below us. Remarkably, our planet fully spins on its axis daily, and if you were near the equator, you would be moving at 460 meters per second or roughly 1,000 miles per hour! The Earth does this while also moving around the sun at 30,000 meters per second or 67,000 miles per hour![1] Wow! Hold on to your seat! Incredibly, our whole solar system is also moving around the Milky Way, in our own spherical galaxy. This is why we can get a glimpse of the Milky Way on clear nights during certain times of the year. It is a wonder that on Earth we don't get dizzy or feel any "g-factors" of movement at any time, but thankfully, that's due to the "gravity of our situation."

Earthrise

The fact that we can live on planet Earth as it is spinning so fast while moving through the solar system is amazing. This feeling is enhanced for those lucky enough to be astronauts looking back on our home from outer space. Viewing Earth this way certainly creates a lasting impression. In her book, *Back to Earth: What Life in Space Taught Me About Our Planet and Our Mission To Protect It*, my friend and astronaut, Nicole Stott, reflects on the iconic Earthrise photo taken on the Apollo 8 mission in 1968. "They were the first to witness in person the beautiful spectacle of our colorful planet, full of life and set against the stark and seemingly endless black backdrop of space, rising in stunning contrast above the lifeless surface of the moon. This single image forever shifted humanity's perspective on who we are and our place in the universe—a simple yet powerful reminder of the undeniable reality of our ultimate interconnectivity and interdependence. We are all Earthlings." When Nicole peered out the window of the spacecraft on her recent voyage and looked back on Earth herself, she said, "the perspective offered through the windows of the spacecraft was so overwhelmingly impressive and beautiful that it far exceeded my highest expectations. No picture, no video and no conversation with others who had flown before could have prepared me for what I saw with my own eyes and felt with my own soul. . . . All the Earth's colors glowed with an iridescence and translucence I'd never seen before." She went on to say, "An Earthrise moment is any moment that stands out for you and impresses you with a sense of awe and wonder that inspires you in a life changing way. Here on Earth we are surrounded every day by opportunities to experience life changing awe and wonder if we are open to it."[2]

From Earthrise to Oceanrise

I had the pleasure of meeting Nicole through a mutual colleague. While she was explaining this Earthrise phenomenon to me, I shared that I'd had a similar experience, not by venturing into outer space—but by traveling into deep inner space. During my career at the Harbor Branch Oceanographic Institute (HBOI), I had the good fortune to experience over five deep dives in manned submersibles, descending over 2,000 feet below the ocean surface. These adventures created feelings of awe and wonder similar to what she had described. Our shared experiences bonded us and led to us being friends ever since, joined by the inner and outer space Earthrise experiences and our common interest in helping inspire people to protect the environment on our spaceship Earth.

J. Seward Johnson of the Johnson and Johnson Company, and Ed Link, who engineered the Link Trainer for pilot training simulation, founded and privately funded HBOI in 1971. It was at HBOI that they built three manned submersibles for inner-space science exploration which could operate at depths previously available only to unique navy vessels and submariners. These subs were remarkable and carried two pilots and two scientists inside an acrylic sphere located in front of an aluminum chamber. This vessel actually looked like a yellow submarine pushing a giant fishbowl. Picture a clear sphered helicopter but traveling underwater to explore the deep sea, while wearing shorts, a tee shirt, and sandals. Fortunately for me, diving in inner space did not take years of practice and training like it does to be an astronaut. Thanks to these manned submersibles and trained submarine pilots it only took a few hours of instruction for me to observe as a scientist.

HBOI had seven different operating divisions at the time, and three that were directly involved with my trips into the deep. The Marine Operations Division did great work designing, building, and maintaining the submersibles. I was the Director of the Aquaculture Division, and then there was Dr. Shirley Pomponi, the Director of the Biomedical Marine Research Division that explored the deep sea for organisms capable of harboring bioactive compounds for medical use.

So, what was I, an aquatic farmer who worked on scaling up the production of clams, oysters, fish, and corals, doing on board a submersible? Well, it turns out that Dr. Pomponi knew that if they discovered a bioactive compound in a rare deep-sea organism, they could not just harvest them until there were none left. Furthermore, if they could not chemically reproduce that compound in a laboratory, they would then have to culture and produce it in large enough amounts to extract the quantities needed for the medical community. Consequently, I was asked to go on some of the expeditions because of my experience in keeping many types of marine organisms alive in captivity and growing them at scale. I got the chance to go to inner space and explore the living "final frontier."

Similar to witnessing an Earthrise from outer space, it was thrilling to experience an *oceanrise* and seeing our planet from a different perspective in the process. The submersible experience has similarities to a spaceship in that it also has a support team on the surface of the Earth and the vessel itself has life support systems that allow us to spend time totally self-contained on the bottom of the ocean. However, the submersible launch took place from the back of an oceanographic ship using an A-frame lift. It was spectacular in that it was a calm, slow-motion dip into the blue—very different from a rocket blasting off into space. Sitting in the front, inside of the 5-foot diameter acrylic sphere, was the main pilot at the controls and the lead scientist of that dive. This was like being in a large fishbowl, only with humans on the inside and fish on the outside.

Into the Deep

What happens next is truly amazing. Once the acrylic sphere enters the water, it seems to completely disappear and you are left with only the water in front of you. This is so startling, and most first-time passengers immediately reach out and touch the sphere, making sure it is still there. For me, this happened every single dive. Once securely in the water, the submersible is disconnected from the ship and the self-controlled, untethered descent out of the blue and into the dark begins. Watching the hull of the ship quietly fade away on the surface of that water must be like seeing the Earth shrink behind a space-bound rocket, but not as fast, furious, or loud.

Migrations and Movable Feasts

Traveling over a couple thousand feet down is not a totally slow descent, as that would take away from valuable bottom-time where the exploration and real work begins. Furthermore, the cost of $10,000 a day, back then, was too expensive to waste with a slow-motion drop below. This journey down did, however, allow us to experience the nightly phenomenon that is the largest living organism migration on Earth.

Night and day in the ocean have more to do with how deep or far away you are from surface sunlight than the actual time of day. The migration of certain organisms in the ocean takes place daily as they rise toward the surface and then head back down, in a rhythm of sorts. But the migrations are not really about travel; they are more like movable feasts. Phytoplankton will migrate up to the photic zone (where light is) to allow for photosynthesis. Algal-eating organisms like zooplankton then migrate toward the phytoplankton to satisfy their nutritional needs. Migrations of fish follow along and gulp quantities of the zooplankton. As the cycle continues, these fish will then find themselves in the bellies of fish-eating predators. Deepwater creatures may just lie in wait for prey or gobble the remains of the daily migration feasts that slowly trickle down to their dark world.

Changing Light and Changing Life Forms

As you descend towards the depth of 500 feet, you start to see the loss of daylight, with most of the colors in the blue, indigo, and violet wavelengths being filtered out by the high column of water now above. Traveling further down towards 1,000 feet mimics the sun going down at night, but without any sunset colors. Once you have gone down 1,000 feet or more, it is pitch black. It is very eerie with no light at all—until the best part happens.

Like the stars coming out at night, the fabulous light-emitting organisms that are the rule in this part of the ocean, rather than the exception, become apparent. This bioluminescence is light that is biologically produced by organisms that have evolved in the sunless world. Small dots sparkle like distant stars, and then large flashes of light, from who knows what, paint the seascape—perhaps a response to something out there being startled by the sub. These strange bioluminescent life forms remind me of the cantina scene from the first Star Wars movie—crazy-looking creatures that only a science fiction creator could imagine. Most had larger than life teeth or mouths, and light emitting organs of some sort to dangle in front of any unsuspecting prey, only to gobble them up in one quick bite.

It is also cold down there so things do not happen as quickly as they do near the surface of the ocean. Ocean waters at 2,000–3,000 feet are (near) freezing (average temperature of 4°C or 39°F),[3] whether at the equator or near the poles. The artificial lights on the submersible scared some, but not all—like a deer caught in headlights. On the bottom there were all kinds of deepwater corals, fish, sponges, and other strange invertebrates. The creatures here have never seen the light of day, and they surely have never seen a submersible containing odd-looking humans inside of it. This is their secret world, one that most people will never experience. For creature and human alike, it was a first contact to be remembered.

Brine Pools and Methane Eaters

My fifth and last submersible dive was the strangest of all, and hard to explain to people back on Earth (I mean land). I had the honor to be one of the first to further explore the *brine pools* of the Gulf of Mexico, 2,400 feet below the surface. Geologists, surveying for oil exploration, usually look for salt domes, an accumulation of salt at the bottom of the ocean which can indicate a good location for the collection of natural gas and oil. On one occasion a geologist found something that looked like an underwater lake sitting on the bottom of the ocean. Salt domes can get saturated with ocean water, dissolving much of the salt and creating a solution that is many times the salinity of the ocean. These brine pools can get so dense in salt concentration that they look like a separate liquid body of water, or a dark pond, sitting on the bottom of the sea (Image 13.1).

The brine pool that I was able to explore was even more incredible than most, as it was surrounded by a ring of strange living creatures like those found in thermal vents. The creatures were not living in the liquid of the brine pool but surviving outside of it—like on a beach near the shore. These newly discovered mussels, worms, and invertebrates live on the nutrition supplied by the methane gas that dissolves in the brine and emanates from it. Close proximity to the methane can be deadly so it's a balancing act for these creatures—far enough away to get the oxygen they need from the water and close enough to feed off the methane.

You may wonder, "How do they get nutrition from the methane?" It turns out there are specific bacteria that can

Image 13.1
A brine pool in the Gulf of Mexico. On the left is the sandy ocean floor that looks like a beach on the edge of a lake, complete with a shoreline containing some mussels. To the right is the brine pool made of dense, super salty water. Photo credit: NOAA.

take methane and turn it into usable carbohydrates. Organisms around brine pools harbor these bacteria on their gills, and the bacteria will share the carbohydrates in return for a place to live. This is similar to how the coral polyp uses the nutrients produced by the zooxanthellae. Don't you just love symbiotic relationships?

My goal for this expedition was to harvest some of the mussels to see if I could get them to spawn, and therefore figure out their sexual reproduction strategy. We were able to successfully gather some of the mussels with the submersible manipulator arm, similar to the one on the International Space Station, and conduct mussel culture experiments in very deep inner space. We collected them into specialized containers on the outside of the sub and produced fertilized eggs a few stages into their development, but not all the way to fully developed larvae. We had, however, *spawned where no man had spawned before.* It may not have been as far away as outer-space travel, but it was just as exciting; maybe even more so due to the all the incredible life forms that live in the deep sea.

This ocean frontier is still a very secret world. Dr. Paul Snelgrove said it best: "We know more about the surface of the Moon and about Mars than we do about [the deep sea floor], despite the fact that we have yet to extract a gram of food, a breath of oxygen or a drop of water from those bodies."[4] During the years that HBOI conducted deep sea exploration with their subs, they discovered on average one new species every single day of sub operations. It is hard to believe that they are not active today due to lack of support and funding. In fact, the ships that carried the subs were sold to private industry to search for oil (fossil fuel). Is your head spinning or is it just the Earth?

A Moment for Deepwater Corals

Although we only went down a little over 2,000 feet in the submersible, corals can be found up to 20,000 feet (6,000 meters) below the ocean's surface. In fact, scientists have discovered nearly as many species of deepwater corals (also known as cold-water corals) as shallow species. There are over 3,300 identified species of deep-sea corals, with more being discovered as more of the depths of the ocean are explored.[5]

Mentioned earlier, there is not much sunlight at 500 feet and none to be found below depths of 1,000 feet. For deepwater corals, this is not a problem. They have not only adapted to the colder temperatures, but they have no zooxanthellae. Without zooxanthellae to provide needed carbohydrates, deepwater corals must filter feed for all of their nutrition. Cold, deep water does not mean there is less food available for the coral and other animals, as we see upwellings near the poles to be full of life. But it does mean that coral life this far down is rather slow growing—and by that, I mean very slow. During a cruise on the research submersible Pisces, scientists collected a gold coral colony off the Hawaiian Islands that was over 2,700 years old.[6] When you consider the continuous regeneration of new polyps from the same primary polyp, it is estimated some colonies were actively growing for as long as 40,000 years, and there may be even older corals elsewhere.[7] The scientific community is fascinated with cold-water corals because they may be the longest-lived animals in the ocean.[8] This now allows us to see further into the oceans past using their calcium carbonate skeletons as paleontological evidence of the environment of past multiple millennia.

Like shallow-water corals, a huge benefit of deepwater corals is their ability to provide habitat for other marine life. The terrain at the bottom of the ocean may be considered boring to some compared to shallow reef systems, but the deep ocean accounts for the majority of benthic or bottom habitats of the world. Any solid surface for other invertebrates to attach to becomes a living resource for all life in the area. It is where fish species like to take advantage of crabs, shrimp, and other life forms. Off Alaska, 85% of commercially important fish species are associated with deep-sea coral habitats.[9] So, even though they are slow growing and hidden to most observers, deep-sea corals hold their own cold-facts version of the "secret life of corals."

Unfortunately, while they may be hidden from view, deepwater corals are not hidden from destructive fishing methods. In fact, fishing efforts have specifically focused on these deep coral habitats because that is where the fish live. Damage is caused when boats use bottom trawls to catch the fish hiding within the corals. They trap the fish and plow right through the corals, pulverizing them in the process. Intensive trawling leaves the sea bottom looking like a plowed field and smooths out the bottom sediments, changing the habitat for deep-sea creatures.[10]

Although these fishing methods are unsustainable, they will not be halted until there are no fish left to economically harvest or governments close these areas to these destructive fishing methods. Both orange roughy, found off the Oculina coral banks from Florida to the Carolinas, and Chilean sea bass, found off of the Pacific coasts, are popular species caught using destructive trawls. Sometimes the netless trawl is used first to pulverize the corals so that the fish cannot hide from the nets that will follow. This reminds me of the destructive dynamite fishing practices still used in some places in Indonesia. We must regulate and protect these areas as preserves, or at least only allow sustainable, non-habitat destroying fishing practices. Thankfully, much of the East Atlantic Oculina Reef areas have been protected, but there have been recent efforts to open them back up to fishing. You can help by making good choices about the seafood you consume and by actively supporting the protection of these deep-sea coral habitats.

14

Community Communication

RESEARCH ON land plants and animals has essentially been taking place since the dawn of mankind as they are easily accessible and part of our everyday life. Recent work has illustrated the fact that plants can communicate with each other and with members of the animal kingdom in various and subtle ways. By 1997, Suzanne Simard had discovered that forest trees share and trade food via fungal networks that connect their roots. Her research on "the wood wide web" made the cover of *Nature*. Suzanne and her colleagues' continued research showed that the wood wide web is like a brain and can communicate information throughout the entire forest, that trees recognize their offspring and nurture them, and that lessons learned from past experiences can be transmitted from old trees to young ones.[1]

I have often wondered if there is a similar "coral-wide web." Our ability to conduct research on corals has taken place only very recently compared to the amount of time we have been able to research plants. As research on coral communication moves into the future, I suspect we will continue to be fascinated by these unique creatures. So, the existence of a coral-wide web seems apparent, but the way it works is still being discovered.

When people think of communication, they typically think of using sense organs—eyes, ears, nose, tongue, and skin—to transfer information to and from their brains. Less developed creatures like corals have none of these, so how do they sense anything? As discussed in Chapter 11, flume tests provide evidence that while traveling to find their final home, tiny coral larvae can somehow detect color and smell the reef water. They are not even polyps yet, but they can still sense certain factors that help ensure their survival.

Coral polyps have a simple nervous system called a *nerve net*. This network of nerve cells (neurons) is relatively unspecialized compared to neurons of higher animals. The nerve net is continuous between individual polyps so any changes felt by a polyp can be transferred from nerve endings through the net.[2] These simple nerve endings provide polyps with the capability to experience the world and sense their environment, similar to our sense of smell and taste. For example, polyps can detect certain substances such as sugars and amino acids, which enables them to detect prey.[3] Also, tiny sensors in the ends of nematocysts in polyp's tentacles trigger the nematocyst to eject when they are stimulated either chemically or physically.[4]

The nerve net allows polyps to sense and communicate basic information among members of the colony, but this cannot be the only way corals communicate. We know that communication takes place between coral polyps and the microbes and zooxanthellae that live with them. Polyps can also communicate with each other, and coral colonies seem to be able to communicate on some level with other coral colonies. Coral colonies have even been shown to communicate with animals. All this communication adds up to more than just a nerve net.

So, what is happening? How does this "talking" occur? Is it through chemical signals or perhaps sound? Next, we will look at other ways coral may be communicating with the understanding that this is an emerging field of research with more questions than answers at this time.

Communication Between Members of the Coral Holobiont

Remember from Chapter 2 that the coral *holobiont* is the polyp (animal), the zooxanthellae (plant inside the polyp), and the microbiome (microbes that live on the outside of the polyp), all living together as one organism—three in one. These three parts are critical to the life of the coral holobiont, so it is believed they must somehow communicate with each other. Does the animal part communicate with the zooxanthellae and the microbes? Do the zooxanthellae and the microbes communicate with each other? How does communication take place when there are no apparent specialized tissues for transmitting information, such as specialized nerve cells, brains, blood vessels, or lymphatic systems? Furthermore, there are no physical structures that we are aware of for transmitting or receiving information.

Yet we know sufficient communication does take place—enough to trigger reactions among the members of the coral. For example, during a bleaching event, is it the polyp animal signaling the algal cells to "Get out!" or is it the algae sending a signal to the polyp to "Please puke us out!" We know a polyp will quickly retract its extended tentacles when a simple shadow is cast over it. But how does the polyp "see" the shadow? Who is signaling for this behavior? The algae might be able to sense the lack of sunlight but how does it tell the polyp so quickly? One theory is that the microbial community plays a major part in this communication process. The microbial community is a continuous covering over the surface of the polyp and could be considered a surface network of receptors and transmitters. Perhaps chemical signaling along this network facilitates communication.

Communication Between Polyps in a Colony

Most coral behavior, such as feeding, defense, and reproduction, is geared for ensuring survival. For feeding, corals have both the plankton capture response and the algal farming mechanisms. For prey capture in a colony, there are many hungry mouths and lots of competition for plankton that float by. Sometimes the more aggressive or bolder polyps get the bigger portion. What if a bold polyp captured a nice copepod (a small crustacean) that took a while to consume, would the neighboring polyps expect it to share? Or, would the benefit to the bold polyp of eating the entire copepod somehow spread to the polyps next door or even the whole colony? We know trees can share nutrition with other trees through their root systems.[5] But what about corals? The stomachs of similar colonial reef animals called zoanthids are interconnected, allowing them to transfer nutrients.[6] Stony coral polyps do not have connected stomachs, but whether they have a way to transfer nutrients among each other is yet to be determined.

It is fascinating that coral polyps from one colony can "recognize" each other as being the same—they are clones of each other. If a colony breaks and a fragment falls away and then starts to grow back towards the colony, the colony recognizes it and fuses with it, making it a part of the colony once more. But if another coral of a different genotype grows too close to that colony, the colony will defend its turf. Sometimes a war will break out, as discussed in Chapter 12. So, how can the colony recognize friend or foe in terms of other coral colonies? In the case of the polyps from broken fragments of their own colony, they are essentially saying, "Hey, you are my identical twin, I can see your DNA!" But how can they know this? Researchers are still trying to figure this out.

As you will read about in Chapter 20, coral colonies do not sexually reproduce until the colony reaches a certain size. There is something telling these polyps, "we are now the size of an adult, let's start acting like one." Somehow, they first get the memo to start producing gametes, and then another one to start spawning. Who or what sends the memos? My bet is on the microbial community that is common to them all. Simple to say but harder to comprehend. We do know that microbial communities have what is called *quorum sensing*, which could be in play here.

Quorum sensing is a mechanism that allows bacteria to talk to each other using chemical signals they produce. Using these signals, they know when their population reaches a particular size. When this happens a change is triggered that benefits the group as a whole. Essentially, quorum sensing allows bacteria to act as an enormous multicellular organism and accomplish tasks they could never accomplish as individuals because they are too tiny. This includes virulence, where they wait until they reach a certain population density before they all release a toxin in unison, resulting in an amount that can actually harm the host. Bioluminescence in the marine bacteria *Vibrio harveyi* is another example. When cells are low in number there is no light, but when they grow to a certain threshold all the bacteria turn on the lights together.[7] Other bacterial activities including biofilm formation and the production of secondary metabolites, such as antibiotic compounds, growth hormones, and pigments—all regulated by quorum sensing.[8,9]

What this means for corals is that bacteria in their microbiome may chemically signal for change within their own community. The signals could be received by the polyps as well, and once recognized has the potential to trigger changes in secretions, enzymes, hormones, or behavior. Coral polyps are connected to each other by the tissue

layer known as the *coenosarc*, which also contains zooxanthellae and the microbiome layer—it connects all members
of the coral colony. With this in mind, could the microbial community be signaling to the polyps that their population is now large enough for the polyps to breed? The
actual spawning could then be triggered by the microbes
sending signals across the entire colony, thus the theorized
coral-wide web. We know trees can communicate with
pheromone type chemicals. And we know microbes can
signal other microbes with pheromone type chemicals, so
maybe they can signal the coral polyps as well.

Communication Between Coral Colonies

When one coral colony starts releasing gamete bundles in
a synchronized fashion, adjacent and nearby colonies (that
are not touching each other) also start releasing their gamete
bundles. You would think the polyps of one colony would be
thoroughly focused on their own spawning and not be concerned with signaling their neighbors to join in the show. In
the blink of an eye though, this triggering and release is faster
than the Rockettes kicking up their feet at Radio City Music
Hall—and just as beautifully choreographed. So, how do coral
colonies across the reef know when it is time to all spawn
together? It is a mystery. Perhaps the microbial community
also plays a part in this colony-to-colony coordination during
spawning events or maybe there are sound signals only they
can hear. The notion that corals can communicate with each
other through sound is a relatively new idea. Through DNA
sequencing amplification (PCR), researchers have found evidence of sound-related genes in corals, suggesting that they
could use sound to interact with their surroundings. What
corals may talk about has yet to be researched, but if it is similar to plants, they most likely communicate about possible
dangers, resources, or other information.[10]

Coral to Animal Communication

It has been shown that corals have the ability to communicate with fish through chemical signals. The research team led by the Georgia Institute of Technology's Mark Hay discovered that coral polyps from the species *Acropora nasuta* emit chemical signals when a certain toxic species of seaweed encroaches on their territory. Reef-dwelling gobi fish respond quickly to the coral chemical signal by eating or moving the seaweed, clearing it away from the coral. To further investigate this, researchers placed filaments of a species of seaweed that is chemically toxic to corals in contact with them. Within a few minutes two species of gobies moved to the site of contact and began neatly trimming away the offending seaweed. Researchers took water samples to determine whether the fish were reacting to the presence of the seaweed or to a chemical signal from the coral. It turns out that the gobies were drawn to the water from damaged corals, but didn't react to the chemical signature of the seaweed by itself. The gobies were being "called" to the area damaged by the seaweed and the signal was coming directly from the damaged coral, not from the seaweed.[11]

The gobies responded within minutes of smelling the chemical cue, which means the signaling done by the corals is incredibly fast. In addition, researchers determined the gobies reduced the volume of seaweed by 30 percent over just three days, effectively containing the threat and reducing coral damage by about 80 percent. Think about it: a coral in danger not only sounds the alarm, but targets the messaging to fish capable of responding quickly and effectively enough to save the day. Anyone can scream for "Help" from a corner when their house is on fire; corals know to call the fire department.

PART III

A New Hope for Corals

15

Yesterday's Extinctions: Five Previous Episodes of Coral Hide-and-Seek

L ET'S START with some earth history, or should I say "ocean" history? Corals have experienced a checkered past of here today and gone tomorrow—and then here again. However, the actual time between such events is millions of years. Corals first appeared approximately 500 million years ago (mya) in the Cambrian Period, during the early Paleozoic Era. Evidence suggests they started as simple solitary organisms, but in response to changes in their environment later evolved to colonial reef builders. Since that time, they have disappeared and then reappeared through the five major mass extinctions on the planet.

The extinctions happened during the following prehistoric times: at the end of Ordovician (445 mya), in the Late Devonian (370 mya), during the Permian–Triassic transition (252 mya), during the Triassic–Jurassic transition (201 mya), and at the end of the Cretaceous—when the Paleogene began—also called the K–Pg (66 mya). Where did they go when they disappeared? Nobody knows. Perhaps they were playing some slow-motion form of hide-and-seek with surviving lineages moving to waters of varying temperature or depth depending on what they needed as the planet's environment changed over time. The corals could do this because much of the environmental change happened over the slow course of hundreds of thousands of years, allowing them enough time to adapt to the changes in the ocean environment.

Some environmental changes happened more quickly though with drastic results, such as the Permian–Triassic extinction caused by huge atmospheric releases of CO_2 from intense volcanic activity. The study of sediments and fossilized creatures show the event was the single greatest calamity ever to befall life on Earth, eclipsing even the extinction of the non-avian dinosaurs. Up to 96% of all marine species perished while more than two-thirds of terrestrial species disappeared. The cataclysm was so severe it wiped out most of the planet's trees, insects, plants, lizards, and even microbes.[1] This extinction is often referred to as the "Great Dying."

The K–Pg (also called the K–T) extinction event was brought on very quickly when an asteroid hit the earth, causing dust to block the sun. This, in turn, killed 80% of all species of animals on earth including all the non-avian dinosaurs.[2] Although some coral species did become extinct during these five extinction events, some of their lineage carried on and has survived through modern day. The fact that they disappeared from the fossil record for long periods of time and then reappeared long down the road is quite remarkable and speaks to the tenacity and resilience of our little friends.

Geologists have divided the last half a billion years into three time eras: the Paleozoic (540–248 mya), the Mesozoic (248–66 mya), and the Cenozoic (the past 66 mya). The transitions between these eras are marked by the profound effects of the mass extinction events mentioned earlier, which is starkly reflected in the fossil record. During the Paleozoic Era, there appeared to be three major biological groups (classified as orders) of calcified corals—two of which went in decline in the middle of the Paleozoic Era and extinct during the Permian–Triassic mass extinction event. The third biological order, Scleractinians, that are still here today, were the prede-cessors of our "hard" or "stony" modern corals.

Unfortunately, we can only track corals in the fossil record when they are calcified and leave a fossil skeleton as evidence. The soft-bodied forms leave a poor record, if any at all. It has been theorized that the gaps in the fossil record occurred because coral abundance was so low during the extinction events that they eluded fossil records all together. Perhaps the survivors were in isolated refuge areas or existed as forms that had no hard skeletons and therefore fossilized poorly.[3] These changes in coral diversity and abundance during the Earth's long history may represent only partial extinctions as there was a continuum of soft-bodied forms that later evolved to have calcium carbonate skeletons again in this game of hide-and-seek.

We've Only Been Dancing on this Earth for a Short While

Playing hide-and-seek during extinction events is not a game though, more of an extreme survival strategy. Today we should look ahead to when the next mass extinction will happen. Are we on the threshold of the next one already? We are living in a unique time in Earth's history, as we are seeing environmental changes happen, not in epochs, eras, or peri-ods, but in decades within our lifetime.

So where are we today, relative to the history of the geo-logical time scale? Technically, we are still in the Cenozoic Era but in the Quaternary Period.[4] We are also considered to be in the Anthropocene Epoch, which is an unofficial unit of geologic time used to describe the most recent period in Earth's history when human activity started to have a signif-icant impact on the planet's climate and ecosystems.[5] The "Man-*messed*-it-up-ocene" Epoch if you will, although you may insert your own favorite verb for *messed*.

To illustrate this, let's envision a time scale not with a watch, or a calendar, but with a yardstick the size of a skyscraper. If the history of Earth was the size of the Empire State building, most of the main part of the building would represent the period of time before life began. Then, moving up this timeline, the uppermost floors would hold the first primitive living organisms—this is where corals started. Remarkably, it is the antenna on the top of the Empire State building that represents the start of what we may think of as higher life forms above single-celled organisms. If we could put an ice cream cone on top of the antenna, that would represent the time when our early human ancestors came on the scene. A fly, sitting on the top of an ice cream cone, on the antenna on the top of the Empire State Building, represents recorded history. For this geologic time scale analogy, our modern world that runs on fossil fuels would be represented by a mere speck of dust on the head of that fly. So much progress has been made in such a short time to create our modern world, but this progress has come with a cost.

Time moves forward essentially in a straight line, so it is easy to visualize geologic time running alongside the Empire State Building. Changes in the earth's environment, though, are typically not linear and are better represented with curves. Image 15.1 shows how the amount of atmospheric CO_2 has increased over the past 140 years, with a corresponding rise in temperature. The graph rises slowly from the year 1880 but becomes steeper as it approaches 2020. This dramatic rise shows that the rate of change is becoming faster in terms of the amount of CO_2 released into the atmosphere, and with it, a corresponding rise in temperature. So, with the average temperature and amount of CO_2 in the atmosphere both steadily increasing, what does this mean for corals?

A Closer Look at CO_2 in the Air and the Sea

In earlier chapters, the correlation between increases in atmospheric temperature and ocean temperature was briefly discussed, and here we will go into a bit more detail. Remember,

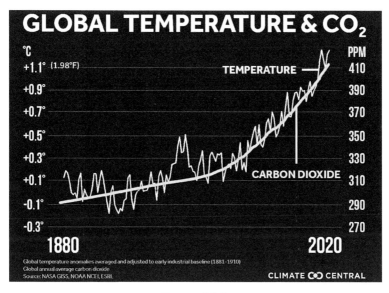

Image 15.1
The rise of temperature and carbon dioxide in lockstep.
Image credit: Climate Central.

as ocean temperatures increase, particularly in the summer months, coral's zooxanthellae partners will leave (or are ejected by) the coral polyp with the result being the polyp then loses a significant source of nutrition. Furthermore, as water temperatures rise, the microbiome on the outside of the coral polyp becomes stressed, leaving the polyp more susceptible to diseases. Unfortunately, that is not all: increasing atmospheric CO_2 levels also creates ocean acidification and sea level rise.

Image 15.2 was created from data taken in Hawaii from 1958–2015. It shows that as the amount of CO_2 in the atmosphere increases (red line), the amount of CO_2 in the oceans also increases (dark blue line), while pH decreases (light blue line)—indicating an ocean that is becoming more acidic (as the level of CO_2 rises in the atmosphere, a large portion becomes dissolved in the oceans, which, in turn, lowers the pH level of the water making it more acidic).

The Struggle for Calcium

The problem of ocean acidification is particularly significant to corals because, as discussed in Chapter 6, calcium naturally binds to acids. Consequently, when the ocean becomes more acidic, corals must work harder to pull calcium out of the water to make their skeletons. They then also need to spend more of their energy producing and maintaining those skeletons, which means that they have less energy for growing or reproducing. Over time the acidic conditions will cause their skeletons to become thin and weak, making them more vulnerable to lurking predators. There is even the future risk that the water around the polyps may become so acidic that the outer skeleton just dissolves, leaving the polyp totally exposed to predation and certain death. Other aquatic species with calcium carbonate shells and exoskeletons, such as clams, oysters, lobsters, and crabs, face similar threats from ocean acidification.

The oceans, back before the rapid release of CO_2 into the atmosphere, seemed to rest at a pH of about 8.3 (the middle of the scale is 7). Presently, we're already down to an average of 8.1, which may not seem too extreme until you factor in studies that show severe skeletal dissolution for polyps beginning at a pH of about 7.7.[6] Now consider that the current reading of 8.1 is merely an average. Some canals and inshore waters around the world, including the canals around the Florida Keys where I work, are already showing a pH reading of under 8.0. If that drops much further, then try as they might to produce a skeleton, all of the polyps in those regions will be reduced to little fleshy tubes, naked, and at the mercy of any fish that comes by looking for an evening meal.

Things Can Get Deep Quickly

If rising sea temperatures and ocean acidification were not bad enough, corals may also suffer due to the increased depths they're now being forced to inhabit. As the earth warms, sea level has been shown to change historically with sea level rise occurring relatively quickly. Image 15.3 shows that sea level has been steadily increasing since 1995, which can be a problem for corals. When corals find themselves with more water above them, it changes the amount of light they receive. This

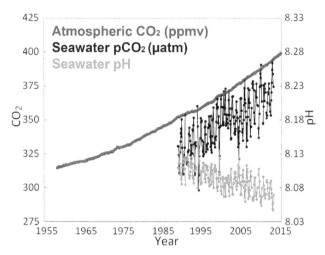

Time series of carbon dioxide and ocean pH at Mauna Loa, Hawaii

Image 15.2

Carbon dioxide and ocean pH levels.

Image credit: NOAA Ocean Acidification Program.

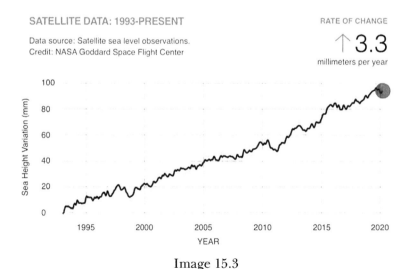

Image 15.3

Recent sea level rise. Image credit: NASA Goddard Space Flight Center.

decrease in light affects the ability of their zooxanthellae to photosynthesize the food products that nourish the polyp. Deeper water also means a drop in temperature with many species unable to tolerate colder water.

Time for a Cool Change

Warming oceans can cause corals to bleach and become more susceptible to disease. A more acidic ocean causes corals to lose their calcium carbonate exoskeletons. Sea level rise puts corals at risk due to loss of light and cooler temperatures. While this scenario sounds apocalyptic (and, for corals, it is), it's much closer at hand than anything described in the book of Revelations.

Today's environmental conditions are pointing towards the next surge of extinctions. The rapid loss of species we are seeing today is estimated by experts to be between 1,000 and 10,000 times higher than the natural extinction rate, also known as the background extinction rate. This rate represents the rate of species' extinctions that would have occurred if we humans were not around.[7]

Looking at the data provided by all three graphs in this chapter, there is no argument that as atmospheric CO_2 rises, the earth warms, the oceans become more acidic, and sea levels rise. Our civilization is currently on the steepest part of the CO_2 curve that unfortunately just looks to be getting worse in the near future. If this upward trajectory indicated out-of-control, unsustainable spending by a corporation, the business in question would make specific and drastic changes to ensure its own future. Likewise, the time is now to make urgent changes to stop apocalyptic coral loss. Nearly half of the world's corals have already been lost in the last 50–60 years. If we don't act now, and as the rate of this die-off continues to rise, the other half could be gone by the end of the century.

16

The Need to Consider Gloom and Doom

GLOBAL DISASTERS resulting in death and destruction will most likely occur in the future due to continued increases in CO_2 production from all sources. If you multiply the continuing increases in CO_2 production by the ever-growing human population, then add in the unrestricted use of our natural resources, the equation results in gloom and doom for the planet. The Intergovernmental Panel on Climate Change (IPCC) 2021 Report forecasts that by 2030 atmospheric temperatures will increase by 2 degrees Celsius—not for a day, but as an entire yearly average.[1]

What that could equate to is mean extremes of low temperatures in some areas and high temperatures in others. This sounds contradictory, and it is why when climate change was first called "global warming" there were climate change deniers, because there are areas that are experiencing colder winters along with warmer summers. But it is the average for the planet that matters—not the temperature swings in just one town or province. If the average winter temperature is 3°C colder, but the average summer temperature is 5°C warmer, the average yearly temperature would be approximately +2°C warmer. This may not sound like much, but +2°C in the summer could make a world of difference to corals, as well as to all of us who live on land.

Problematic Rates of Change

The earth has always been heating up some and cooling down some, and we know from the wide geographic disbursement of fossils that corals can survive at higher temperatures. So, one might think, if oceans are getting a little warmer now, no problem, right? Wrong. The issue (at least for corals) isn't how much the temperature of the ocean is changing, but rather, how quickly the rate of change is happening. Given enough time, many thousands of years for example, corals and other animals have been able to adapt to these gradual shifts, thus improving their ability to survive in their new environment. This has happened in the recent past. The Red Sea is a long thin seawater inlet of the Indian Ocean, lying between Africa and the Middle East. It passes between the hot deserts of both and is unique in that it is very warm relative to other seas. The Red Sea, however, has flourishing coral reefs. These corals are able to thrive because they had tens of thousands of years to evolve and acclimate.

Currently, however, there is no long time period to evolve and acclimate for the rest of the coral reefs around the world, and this could very well cause the sixth mass extinction in our Earth's history. The amount of carbon dioxide and other greenhouse gases that we are releasing are comparable to those seen in prior mass extinctions.[2] This is no small thing—the "Great Dying" mass extinction event that occurred 252 million years ago was caused by rapid global warming. During this event up to 96% of marine species on the planet and two-thirds of the terrestrial species disappeared.[3] Anybody who says that humans will be able to survive the future that we are actively creating right now is, at best, foolishly optimistic and, at worst, criminal in their spreading of misinformation.

Triggering Events and Tipping Points

One of the more compelling theories about mass extinctions, developed by George Curvier in the early 1800s, is known as "Catastrophism." In essence, Curvier believed the gaps of life found in the fossil record were the result of mass extinctions caused by catastrophic events that altered the way life developed and rocks were deposited.[4,5] He turned out to be right about this.

Today we have global ecological pressure in terms of a rapidly warming climate, rising sea levels, and increasing oceanic acidity. At the moment, however, we do not have any large triggering event associated with mass extinctions affecting us, such as high volcanic activity or meteor strikes. But that could change, and it could change quickly.

The slow attrition of species from the world's ecosystems without some sort of a major triggering event may not be enough to cause a mass extinction event if other species have time to adapt to the changing conditions. The problem with human-caused climate change, however, is that it is a sustained ecological pressure that will also likely cause a triggering event. The triggering event can then create a cataclysmic tipping point that may lead us into the sixth mass extinction.

For example, there are massive stores of methane, a greenhouse gas many times more powerful than carbon dioxide, trapped underneath ice sheets in the Arctic called permafrost. The permafrost covers 24% of the surface of land masses in the northern hemisphere and accounts for nearly half of all organic carbon stored within the planet's soil. As long as this organic matter remains frozen, it will stay trapped in the permafrost. However, if it thaws, microbes will begin to eat the material, causing it to decay and release carbon dioxide and methane into the atmosphere.

Permafrost temperatures are rising at a much faster rate than the temperature of the air in the Arctic, and have risen between 1.5 to 2.5°C in the last 30 years.[6] Even if a small fraction of these greenhouse gases are released in a short amount of time, it will have major consequences on not only the Arctic, but Earth's entire climate system, as global climate change will intensify. The melting of the permafrost is one example of a triggering event that could eventually be enough to push us past the point of no return (a tipping point) and cause a mass extinction event.

Look Up, Look Down

Don't Look Up, a film written and directed by Adam McKay and starring Leonardo DiCaprio and Jennifer Lawrence, was released towards the end of 2021. The movie is a satirical, dark comedy about a planet-killing comet that is hurtling towards Earth. According to McKay, the comet stands as a metaphor (not a meteor) for the climate crisis, which is also lethally impacting our planet. The film is centered on distraught scientists who are scrambling to get politicians, the media, and the general public to believe them about the incoming comet, and the impending doom for the planet.[7] Their hope is that action will be taken to set the comet off course, thus saving the planet.

As a metaphor about the climate crisis, the film is accurate in that this planet-changing phenomenon is being ignored by some, discredited by many, and even debated politically whether it exists or is just partisan politics at play. If we knew a comet was heading towards our planet, and that its inevitable impact would possibly end life as we know it, hopefully we would take some action. Likewise, we should also consider the similar impact we should be bracing ourselves for from the enormous amount of clear gas (CO_2) continuously being released into our atmosphere.

Don't Look Up should inspire us to take climate change much more seriously. There could be a similar movie called *Don't Look Down* to encourage us to consider what is happening under our oceans regarding climate change that is hidden from our everyday lives. The ability to "see" the impacts of climate change may not really be the issue though, as hurricanes, droughts, fires, and the melting of glaciers that are above the water are not really hidden from the view of the public. Yet there still is too much debate and even worse, denial. Too much "bla-bla-bla" or "all talk-no action" as one young climate activist likes to say. "Words that sound great but so far have not led to action; our hopes and ambitions drown in their empty promises," chimes activist Greta Thunberg.[8]

What if Bleaching Took Place on Land?

Consider coral bleaching, a brutal condition where the loss of the algal plants from the coral organism makes the coral look stark white. Coral bleaching can literally happen overnight. Now, imagine if this happened on land. You walk outside in the morning one day and every green plant has turned white. Not just one kind of flowering plant in your garden, but the grass, trees, shrubs, and hedges, all turned white. It would certainly be a wake-up call and hopefully a call to action.

As we saw in previous chapters, bleaching events on the reefs were thought to be a once-in-a-century occurrence, like a hundred-year flood. Unfortunately, these floods are now becoming almost yearly occurrences in some areas. Similarly, massive coral bleaching events have accelerated their own global pace, and now take place multiple times per decade with some back-to-back incidences. Even World Heritage

Areas like the Great Barrier Reef are not immune from these disasters.

Boom Goes the Reef

Climate change is the top stressor for coral reefs and all life on the planet, but there are plenty of others as well. All introduced by humans, these may differ from one area to another. One example is dynamite fishing. In this practice, dynamite and other explosives are used to send shock waves through the water, stunning or killing fish which are then collected and sold. This also destroys the reefs in the areas where it takes place. It is hard to hide the noise of dynamite being set off—even underwater. Yet dynamite fishing still occurs in parts of the world and does so without the other fishermen taking action against those destroying their fishing grounds. Hardware supply store owners in these areas have been known to sell the explosives to fishermen knowing what they were going to use them for. Laws to protect these reefs should be enacted and enforced by either marine officers or natural resource managers.

Now or Later

What is the right answer for coral restoration? Should we first try to stop the stressors before starting the restoration? When it comes to the stressor of dynamite fishing the answer is a definitive "Yes!" But the answer is not so clear cut when it comes to other stressors. Many people, including some restoration ecologists and natural resource managers, believe the answer to the above question is almost always that we should stop the stressors before starting restoration. Others suggest creating marine protected areas and have Mother Nature take care of the restoration on her own terms. I do not believe either of these approaches will work. If we wait until we stop all the stressors before starting any restoration, or leave everything to Mother Nature, it will be too late. Would you like a physician to tell you he is not going to restore your breathing or stop your bleeding until he has everything else about your health figured out?

Passive restoration strategies have not worked well on natural land-based systems because there still exists a big problem—us. Or should I say too many of us, here at the same time, for a natural system to ever fully recover. We are approaching 8 billion humans on this planet, where only an estimated 107 billion have ever lived.[9] Many have fantasies about one day going to Mars, where there is no life and no (usable) water, and literally leaving this world's worries behind. But unless about 4 billion more of us also get off, it only buys us one more generation before we get back to a "too-many-people-for-the-planet-to-be-sustainable" situation. Our global trajectory does not look good according to the 234 scientists that read over 14,000 research papers to produce the 2021 IPCC report. The multiple alternatives and projections discussed did not paint a rosy picture. In fact, the changes in climate we are already seeing are unprecedented in recent history and will affect every region of the globe.[10] We have to change in order to stop the climate from changing, and we can if we so choose.

Restoration

What we should do as a society is shift away from our reliance on fossil fuels since the consumption of these products directly releases enormous amounts of CO_2 into the atmosphere. In addition, we need to: 1) undo as much damage from CO_2 emissions and other pollutants as quickly as possible and 2) prepare for sea level rise, extreme weather, and climate conditions that will impact all natural resources and food availability. Restoring corals, while not a panacea for the planet, will do a lot to help on both fronts.

First, coral reefs can help combat climate change because they essentially operate as long-term carbon sinks by absorbing carbon in their calcium carbonate exoskeletons that then stays sequestered for ages. The algae inside of the corals use CO_2 in combination with energy from the sun to make carbohydrates for food while also releasing oxygen as a byproduct. That means that the more corals grow, the more CO_2 they remove from ocean water (reducing ocean acidity) while also adding to the overall amount of oxygen in ocean water. Second, coral reefs can help protect our shorelines from rising sea levels and storms by growing upwards as the sea level rises and by absorbing tidal energy. Having healthy coral reefs will also improve and increase our seafood resources.

Since we know that ocean water is becoming warmer and more acidic, we can help repopulate the world's reefs with corals that are more resistant and resilient to these threats. *Resilient* corals can recover from these stressors, while *resistant* corals seem to withstand them altogether and remain unchanged. These resilient and resistant strains of corals do exist, they can be grown in nurseries, and eventually outplanted to help maintain and grow functional working reefs. The addition of these resistant and resilient strains may help other species on the reef survive potential extinctions by providing a functioning habitat for them to live.

Restoring coral reefs is critically important because they are the underwater forests where so many other creatures live. There are hundreds of fish and thousands of invertebrate species that depend on a healthy living coral reef for their existence. They are one of the backbones of oceanic biodiversity, supporting all forms of life in our tropical seas. We now have the technology to do it, and we can do it at a large enough scale to make a real meaningful difference. But that is only the first half of the battle—now we need the funding, the people, and the organizing skills to help restore corals across the world. So let's get going, while also reducing environmental stressors at the same time. Through focus and commitment, we can all help to shut the door on "gloom and doom."

Lucky Lookdown

Lucky Lookdown is a wonderful children's book by Suzanne Tate about a funny looking fish.[11] This flattened shaped silvery fish species has eyes way above its mouth and therefore always looks as if it is looking down (Image 16.1). In this story, one young fish in a school of lookdowns at the public aquarium is sad because he feels all of the other fish are looking down on him (and of course they are). But the one thing that makes Lucky happy is the children that come to the aquarium to visit.

When I look down under the ocean, I feel lucky to have seen it in its glory. However, I feel sad when I see the loss of corals from their original splendor. And I am still amazed when children, or young people, see a reef for the first time and I hear them say how wonderful it looks. I immediately

Image 16.1
A small school of lookdown fish. These flat silvery fish have eyes that are way above their mouths, giving them the appearance that they are always looking down.

reflect on what it looked like before and what it should look like now, and I am left saddened. Like Lucky, I have to focus on those children and their awe and appreciation of the natural world. The many reefs that I have been fortunate enough to see restored from barren areas back into glorious living reefs by the coral restoration community serve as a gift to the next generation. The children that make Lucky Lookdown happy again are the same ones that give me the drive to continue our work, and they deserve to see the underwater Garden of Eden.

One of the craziest things I have ever seen is a lookdown fish swimming upside down. In many canals in the Florida Keys, people install underwater lights to attract fish for their viewing pleasure at night. It is here where you can sometimes see a very funny fish behavior. The glowing bulb of the underwater light attracts all kinds of sea life and can look as bright as the sun to a fish. Because of this the lookdown fish get disoriented and start to swim upside down looking away from the light they may perceive as the sun. They reorient themselves to swim looking away from the light and therefore upside down.

So, like Lucky Lookdown, we need to keep swimming, with hopeful eyes looking down at the corals under the sea, and to modify our behavior accordingly for corals, the oceans, and ourselves.

There is hope and the next chapter gets us started.

17

Hope, Coral Trees, and Bucket Babies

IN EARLIER chapters I discussed how low the odds are for both fertilization between a coral egg and sperm to take place, and then for the resulting coral larvae to even make it to the stage of a primary polyp. For coral sexual reproduction, it is a numbers game, with a very small number of larvae ever growing into an adult coral colony. Couple that with environmental stressors that severely impact corals, like climate change, and you might ask whether or not there is any hope for corals at all. I am happy to now say that by means of *active coral restoration*, the answer is "YES!" But just like reforestation on land, active coral restoration requires human assistance.

The current practice of active coral restoration has been made possible by the contributions of many dedicated scientists from the 1990s to present day. There was trial and error, some serendipity, game-changer discoveries, and a whole lot of commitment by fabulous people to move active coral restoration forward. Much of the work being conducted to get us to this place was being done simultaneously. For example, in the Florida Keys I was working on sexual reproduction techniques for the massive coral species during the same time period that my colleague, Ken Nedimyer, was working on techniques for asexual reproduction through the breaking or *fragmentation* of coral. Luckily, we, and colleagues around the world, eventually had success. Corals grown in laboratories and in open-water marine nurseries are now created through both fragmentation and sexual reproduction. This allows us to have hope for coral reefs in the future. This pathway for hope will be illuminated in the following sections and chapters.

Coral Trees and Other Devices

Corals naturally reproduce asexually through fission or budding, thus creating more polyps. Another way for corals to reproduce asexually is through fragmenting or breaking of the colony, usually seen in the fragile branching corals. These corals, primarily staghorn corals, can break during severe storm events and the broken pieces that survive will eventually attach back to the substrate and start to grow a new colony. Consequently, scientists followed Mother Nature's lead and started to break off staghorn coral pieces, grow them to a certain size, and then outplant them onto the reef. Scientists started to get creative when figuring out how to grow these branching corals to scale. Nedimyer took it to an art form and a more detailed account of his intriguing story can be found in *Active Coral Restoration: Techniques for a Changing Planet.*[1]

In short, corals can grow on man-made underwater tree-like structures and other unique devices. Staghorn and other branching corals are now typically grown on underwater trees made out of PVC pipe. This practice did not originally start out on trees however, but the evolution of corals being grown on underwater trees came about rather quickly. The start came in the form of concrete or cement blocks, upon which staghorn coral fragments were glued, or cemented, to

the flat-sided surface. These blocks provided a vertical plat-
form, 8 inches (20 mm) above the bottom substrate, which
helped to keep the corals from being covered in sand. This
simple and inexpensive method worked very well until
storms shifted the bottom sands so much that some blocks
were buried or partially buried. This incentivized restoration
practitioners to figure out a way to elevate the coral above the
block so that the coral would not get covered by sand.

The first easy innovation included the use of an additional base made of cement, usually in the form of a round
disc about the size of a drink coaster but thicker. These were
homemade as the industry had not matured enough to moti-
vate their manufacturing. Instead of relying on third parties,
inexpensive molds were secured through actual parties, specifically, keg parties. After the kegger would end, we cleaned
up the mess and gathered all the discarded "red Solo cups" we
could find to make cement "pucks" that would become the
bases to grow the corals—a true win-win. These bases were
the size of hockey pucks, and each was produced by pouring
about 1 inch (25 mm) of cement into the bottom of the cup,
which was then left to cure, or harden, overnight. A slight
pressure on the bottom of the cup the next day freed the perfectly produced puck that would be attached to the cement
block with epoxy or cement. Next, the coral fragment would
be attached to the puck. The Solo cup mold could be used
a number of times before it had to be replaced. Whenever
more pucks were needed, we just looked to find where the
beer flowed like water and offered up our services.

Before long, increasing the height of the corals above the
cement base became an obsession. Various arrangements of
blocks and pucks made the structures look more like cande-
labras so that drifting sand from storms would go through
the spaces in these vertical bases while the living coral sat well
above any risk of being buried alive. Others extended the
height with the use of PVC pipe and these particular nurseries looked like they contained rows of pipe organs holding

the corals 1 or 2 feet (30–60 cm) above the cement slab they were attached to.

This trend of moving the corals higher up into the water column eventually helped to create the structures used today, such as PVC nursery trees, line nurseries, and mid-water racks (Images 17.1, 17.2, and 17.3). Corals were given a figurative "leg-up" and life uptown was now better. We now know that mid-water nurseries can realize up to a 50% faster growth rate than those nurseries on the bottom.[2] Furthermore, these structures look more like legitimate aquaculture production systems. The coral tree is the epitome of modern coral professionalism and scale. The tree is made of a vertical piece of PVC pipe anywhere from 3–9 feet (1–3 m) in length and tethered in place with line or cable to an anchoring device on the bottom. On the top are buoys that also help to hold it upright and in a vertical position. Horizontal extensions made of fiberglass rods, or smaller PVC pipes, become the branch-like structure where the corals are suspended with monofilament line. Once in place it looks like a plastic Christmas tree dangling corals instead of ornaments, so the term *coral trees* seemed appropriate.

Coral trees fit the needs of the corals better than the concrete blocks, and they make nursery maintenance much easier. For the corals, it means being well off the sediments, minimalizing the risk of being buried. At these heights corals are exposed to fantastic water movement from passing currents, which provide more effective diffusion of nutrients, wastes, and gases through the polyp and its zooxanthellae and microbial partners. For the nursery staff, it means easier maintenance, as divers can easily observe, clean, maintain, or harvest corals like apples off of a tree—but no ladder required. The coral trees are both easy and cost effective in that they allow for larger scalable field nursery production.

Across the tropical regions where corals are grown in nurseries, there are other similar structures to grow the corals higher in the water column. From supported wire tables

Image 17.1

Coral trees made from PVC pipe with staghorn coral fragments suspended from the branches. Buoys at the top help to keep the trees vertical. Photo credit: Ken Nedimyer.

Image 17.2

A line nursery with staghorn corals. Fish seem to enjoy hanging around these elevated coral nurseries. Photo credit: Ken Nedimyer.

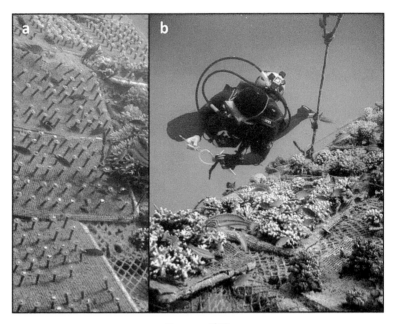

Image 17.3

Coral farming at the Eilat mid-water floating coral nursery: (a) trays or racks with coral fragments glued on plastic pegs and (b) trays with fully developed branching colonies reared at the coral nursery from small fragments. Photo credit: Buki Rinkevic.

to floating nets and lines, there are as many ways to grow a coral in a nursery as there are nursery growers. Many variations are made as either the result of varied access to different materials, the costs of those materials, and/or the ease of maintaining the equipment and structures.

Any good substrate on which coral grows will also be appealing to algae, sponges, barnacles, and any other organism that may wish to settle and fill the habitat. Many coral practitioners have found ways to work with their environment and allow herbivores and other organisms to eat the algae that may overgrow the coral and naturally clean the nursery. This makes for a good balance as long as coral-eating creatures such as parrot fish, coral-eating snails, or brittle worms don't also take advantage of a fresh-farmed meal.

In these open-water coral nurseries, the juvenile corals are taken care of until they are ready to be on their own. Once branching corals have grown to about 10 cm (2.5 inches), or their massive coral counterparts have reached about 3 cm (1.25 inches), they are outplanted onto a reef—a great milestone in active coral restoration. That said, attaining this milestone isn't the end of the restoration effort, as survival, growth, and monitoring should be a part of every coral restoration project. Years of observation should be conducted to document the restoration result, and while that might extend the project's duration, thankfully, true restoration won't require the centuries' worth of recorded observation that was once thought necessary. Outplantings in Belize, Mexico, and Indonesia have shown excellent results in as little as 2–10 years. Results of living coral habitats, and the return of beautiful fish and invertebrates, is no less than miraculous.

Bucket Babies

The early decades of my life were geared towards aquaculture for the food industry, which provided me valuable experience for addressing open ocean and marine system challenges. And, thankfully, much of my success was achieved by providing marine organisms with good water quality and good nutrition, which is not always an easy task. In addition, I helped create nurseries where many of their offspring would survive, unlike in the wild where the odds for survival were not as great. These skills translated well to my work with corals and eventually active coral restoration.

Fortunately, what we now realize is that some strains or genotypes of each coral species may hold more natural resistance or resilience to environmental challenges then others. Resistance in corals is their ability to remain unchanged when being exposed to a disturbance. For example, corals that do not bleach during periods of ocean warming are considered *resistant* to bleaching. Resilient corals have the ability to recover from a disturbance and return to their pre-disturbance state. So, a *resilient* coral may bleach during a period of ocean warming, but over time its zooxanthellae return and the coral regains its health. There are very few populations of corals that are either resistant or resilient to the stressors they face today. If most of the reef dies, even the most resistant or resilient coral strains would be impacted, requiring what could be up to a millennium to reproduce and repopulate the reefs to their former levels. Unfortunately, during the time it takes for coral reefs to restore naturally, we could lose vital fish and invertebrate species that depend on the corals and their habitat for survival. We would have to wait many hundreds or even thousands of years to regain the missing biodiversity of species. Still, my feeling was that the best chance to save coral and keep reefs functioning was to simply select from the reef the most stress resistant and resilient coral strains, grow more of them, and then plant them back onto the reefs. After all, sexually reproduced clams, shrimp, and fish were being produced in hatcheries all over the world.

What I did not know back in 2005 was that coral sexual reproduction in captivity had not yet been successfully achieved at any sizable scale. Originally the thought was that if we could collect gametes and put them in the same buckets without predators and other impediments, many eggs would become fertilized. Having them in proximity like this made it a lot easier for the gametes to find each other, which is very important as fertilization will only take place between the eggs and sperm from different colonies. Then the fertilized eggs would become larvae that could be released back onto the reef, allowing Mother Nature to take care of the rest. But when put into practice there was no real way to tell if any of these larvae made it to adulthood.

Other scientists took this idea a step further. They allowed the larvae to settle on ceramic tiles and grow into polyps.

Then the tiles would be set back onto the reef where growth would hopefully take place. However, this idea did not meet with enough success either. Some scientists would continue to try to grow polyps in a lab for various amounts of time but even then only one or two out of millions would make it. None of these approaches were helping us hit our goal of producing both the numbers and genetic variety needed to help restore our reefs. But science builds upon itself, and these previous efforts helped us determine what the next course of action should be. So, my colleagues and I at the Mote Marine Lab Tropical Research Center, where I was the Executive Director, decided to approach sexual reproduction differently. We focused on providing intensive care for the gametes all the way through stages where high mortality can occur (the *bottlenecks* I like to call them), and essentially assist in the creation of tank-raised test-tube babies, even if it took years to get them to a size where they could survive in the wild.

To do this, we decided to take a targeted approach with elkhorn coral on Looe Key in the Florida Keys. Thirty years ago, Looe Key was full of elkhorn coral, but since then the population had dwindled significantly. There were only two remaining stands of elkhorn on opposite sides of the reef, which obviously were able to resist or bounce back from disease and environmental stressors—after all, they were still here while all the others had died off. Because these elkhorn appeared to have some resistance and/or were resilient to bleaching or disease, we decided to try and sexually reproduce them.

We waited until the predicted spawning event and went out to Looe Key in two separate boats, each going to a separate stand of elkhorn coral quite a distance apart on the reef. When the upside-down snowstorm occurred, our scientist divers collected as many gamete bundles as they could in collection nets and transferred them into buckets (see Image 17.4). Then the boats came together and gametes from the two different

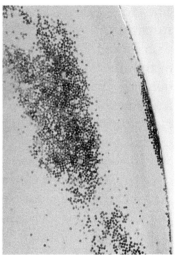

Image 17.4

On the left are simple five-gallon plastic buckets with coral larvae on the surface. The image on the right is a closeup of the floating coral larvae on the surface and sticking to the sides of the bucket. These have to be rinsed off of the sides and kept clean.

elkhorn stands were immediately mixed, as the usually active sperm live for less than an hour.[3] The boats with the buckets returned to the lab on shore for intensive care. From that point, it merely became a matter of making sure that the developing larvae survived. Simple, right? Not exactly.

Changing the Diapers

The days and then weeks right after a bucket spawning event require intensive time and effort to care for these newborn larvae, which I affectionately call coral babies or *bucket babies*. Once in the buckets, some of the eggs and developing larvae would die and rupture, discarding fats in the form of oils that were meant to nourish the developing coral babies.

These fats and oils needed to be removed so they would not affect the living fertilized eggs and larvae. This meant being up most of the night, running around cleaning and changing out the buckets, putting fresh ocean water in them, and stealing what sleep could be had in the lab.

We believed if the water wasn't changed every two hours all the larvae would die. With fat or oils floating in the same location as the viable eggs and larvae, this was not an easy task. We would have to remove the excess oils and decaying eggs, as well as the bacteria trying to feed on them, without removing the viable fertilized eggs or larvae. Dipping out water using a small pipette or dish was time consuming. Instead, we used plastic dishes or film. This worked very well at the swimming larval stage, as the fast-beating cilia of the living larvae kept it from remaining on the plastic film. Meanwhile, the dead eggs and dead larvae, as well as the fats and oils, would stick to plastic wrap. It would look as if we were fighting a bull, not with a matador's red cape, but with clear saran wrap streaming on the surface of the buckets. I affectionately termed these all-night events "changing the diapers" of the coral babies.

It didn't take long to figure out that the coral babies needed clean water to survive, but how to accomplish this without a flowing ocean proved difficult. Even though we were able to get the water we needed in the laboratory from a salt water well, the first time this sexual reproduction run was tried only about 11 test-tube corals survived from tens of thousands of gametes. Over time we fine-tuned our methods and now can consistently raise over a few thousand survivors, which is amazing. In the wild, we'd be lucky if one of these bucket babies matured into adulthood every 10–100 years.

The fact that we can now cultivate coral babies by the hundreds or thousands means that we can create new recombinations of genetic material in each new coral, thereby producing more genetic biodiversity within the species of corals that we are able to grow. This is incredible news because it allows us to hasten the progress of natural selection and create a wider range of new genetic crosses or genotypes that may not only survive but which may be more resilient/resistant to the harsh conditions of today's oceans. Now that we can get them to survive, we need to grow them—and fast!

18

My Eureka Mistake and a
Game-Changer for Corals

THE PROCESS of fragmentation and then regrowth mentioned in the previous chapter was probably first observed
by people with home salt-water aquariums. Aquarists with
branching corals in their tanks could easily and inadvertently
break them while vacuuming or re-arranging the display. In
fact, for corals from the Pacific Ocean, it was standard practice to break them in half to grow, as they were a major part
of the aquarium trade.

In the Atlantic Ocean, elkhorn and staghorn corals (*Acropora palmata* and *Acropora cervicornis*) are the only two species
of branching corals. The rest of the 30 or more species are
the massive corals—mountain corals, boulder corals, brain
corals, etc. Massive corals do not naturally break or fragment
like the branching species do. Massive coral species actually
are what build the majority of the reef structure and habitat,
and provide shoreline protection.

With their large lateral branches, elkhorn coral are considered reef builders as well, but were not fragmented for

restoration purposes. As a result, in Florida and the Caribbean, only the fast-growing but also short-lived staghorn corals were fragmented in the first coral cultivation practices for coral reef restoration. At the time, I referred to all of the other species as *orphan corals* as they were not considered for culture or restoration. They were ignored as candidates for this simple *break-and-multiply* strategy used for the fast-growing staghorn coral.

Fragments of Opportunity

Then hope came for my orphan corals, and in serendipitous fashion. From 2004–2005, the U.S. military was downsizing the naval base in Key West, Florida. Under the guidance of the National Oceanic and Atmospheric Administration (NOAA), they were repairing an old sea wall before returning it to the city. Over a hundred years old, the sea wall had a lot of coral growth on it. A contractor had these corals removed and then replanted at a vessel grounding site. From this removal process, some smaller fragments of coral were generated that could not be handled by the normal transplanting methods they were using at the time, so NOAA offered them to us. These fragments were certainly "fragments of opportunity" as we had been wanting to create a coral gene bank at the Mote Tropical Research Lab in the Florida Keys by obtaining and growing as many diverse species of corals as possible. So, these newly acquired fragments from NOAA were sorted and placed among six glass aquarium tanks to hold in captivity. As scientists, we were not content to just sit and watch corals grow so we conducted experiments to try and figure out different ways to help them to grow faster.

In one study we decided to cut massive-type corals (my orphan corals) to see how fast they would grow back. Starting with 300 fragments of massive corals, we cut them in half. It took them three years to grow back to the original fragment size, which we found discouraging. Their very slow growth rate would make using them for restoration efforts more difficult.

While experimenting with the growth rate of massive corals, I was also observing our first "test-tube" baby elkhorn corals produced a few years earlier in the lab from gametes collected in the field (Chapter 17). The growth rate from the gamete stage seemed even slower than the fragments from the corals of opportunity. Once the test-tube babies had settled as a primary polyp, it took over three years to get to the size of a coin. I felt very discouraged because this growth rate also was way too slow to be a solution for future coral propagation and restoration. Reluctantly, I removed the dozen or so of them from their place of honor on an elevated rack in the middle of the glass tank to the very bottom of the tank.

A Break for Corals

Several months later, I went to move those same corals again to another newly cleaned aquarium and one was stuck to the bottom. I yanked at it, not knowing it had attached itself to the bottom glass. This juvenile coral then broke into a dozen tiny pieces. Thinking that I just killed one of the first surviving test-tube baby corals produced from our larval trials, I was quite upset. Tiny fragments (containing just a few polyps each) remained in the tank and I just left them there with the intention to clean them up later. Two weeks passed before I got around to it. To my surprise, they had survived this accident and actually had grown 25–40 times faster than normal.

I was shocked and more than ecstatic. Not only were they still alive, but they had produced many new polyps in lightning speed! So like any good scientist, I needed to replicate this new phenomenon. Quickly, I grabbed a scalpel, cut them again into small fragments containing just 1–3 polyps each and glued them onto their own cement base. Now these fragments, or better termed *micro-fragments*, were placed back on top of the PVC rack on the very top row.

And just like magic, they did it again! This time they grew much faster than any recorded massive coral species. One small mistake by this man became one large leap for coral-kind. My mistake become known as my *Eureka Mistake*, a term coined by Richard Morin in his article "A Quest to Grow a Coral Reef," published in the *New York Times* in November 2014. This article made it to the front page of the science section. Morin called this error "an absolute game-changer for both the quantity and speed for all of the rest of the coral species, both big and small to be grown." And to think it all happened by my accident! Or perhaps it was divine intervention . . .

Wound Healing

Once our extreme euphoria settled down a bit, we began to wonder what was actually causing this accelerated growth and lateral extension of these micro-fragments. We are still learning and hypothesizing about the answer, but we do know of similar analogies in both the plant and animal world. When the outer branches of a tree are pruned, it is stimulated to grow more branches.

Now when someone asks me, "What causes that, Doc?" I usually tell my own story of how when I was young and learning to skateboard or ride a bike, I would fall from time to time and open up some skin on my knees or elbows. Skin does not grow very fast, but when skin is cut, it immediately starts the process of *wound healing*—first by stopping the bleeding, then forming a scab, then quickly producing brand new skin underneath. Within just a few weeks, full healing has occurred.

This is what we think the coral is doing. Stimulated by a wound-healing process, it quickly produces new polyps, coral tissue, and skeleton. Logically, a sessile animal does not want to give up its territory or get grown over, so this is a beneficial adaptation that seems to be present in every coral, whether massive or branching.

But what would have caused a larger boulder coral or brain coral to react this way? It is not like they are kids riding bikes or are fragile like the branching staghorn corals. It had to be something that had an impact on almost all corals for very many years to encourage the fast wound-healing response. This probably evolved out of necessity—possibly due to the impact of parrot fish bites. Yes, that familiar colorful fish actually eats corals. With a set of enlarged teeth that looks more like a parrot than a fish, they bite off pieces of coral, digest the polyps, and then secrete the remaining calcium carbonate skeleton as white coral sand.

This is not an abnormal occurrence since the beaches in the tropics are full of this beautiful sand. But for the corals, parrot fish are a continuous threat. If those bite holes do not close up and heal quickly, the wounded coral would look like Sponge-Bob Square Pants. If left in this damaged, weakened state for too long, the bitten corals would eventually be colonized by other organisms wanting that valuable space on the reef to settle. Perhaps another coral, sponges, burrowing mollusk, or those colorful feather duster worms would get a foothold. So these corals respond to damage caused by parrot fish bites and other causes by quickly growing tissue to heal the wounded area.

Micro-fragmentation

This "game-changer" for coral restoration means we can simulate the healing response from parrot fish bites by cutting pieces of coral into bite size micro-fragments and letting them grow back quickly. Now termed *micro-fragmentation*, this is the newest, fastest technology used to produce many new coral micro-fragments from parent corals. Before micro-fragmentation, it would normally take 1–3 years to grow a massive coral to the size of a golf ball. We then would cut it in half to create two more corals, wait 1–3 more years again for them to grow back to size and repeat.

With micro-fragmentation technology, we use the same golf ball size coral and cut it into 20–100 tiny micro-fragments, some with only 1–2 polyps each. Not only do we now get large quantities of micro-fragments, but they are each stimulated to grow back to golf ball size in months instead of years.

In our first few years at Mote, it took us 6 years to cut and produce just 600 corals the "old-fashioned way." After my Eureka Mistake, we could cut more than 600 pieces in a day, and they would grow back to the 3-year size in just 6–12 months. Not only were we running out of space, but we could not get tanks to house them in fast enough.

This technique became easy to teach. We were able to get volunteers and students to assist us. To cut the coral into micro-fragments, we used a special diamond bladed band saw. Ironically, this saw was used in the jewelry trade to cut coral skeletons to make bracelets and rings. We adapted it to hold salt water to lubricate the blade and successfully cut tiny pieces of living coral with its fleshy tissue into hundreds of micro-fragments (see Images 18.1 and 18.2).

It took more than a few years for the rest of the established coral science community to acknowledge this phenomenon. On more than one occasion, the skeptics would comment that corals do not grow that fast. "Haven't you read the literature?" they would ask. However, seeing was believing when they came by to visit.

Micro-fragmentation is now the recognized process used in almost every new coral restoration program. In fact, a 2022 article by Donna Stover and her associates offered definitive proof that there is chemical change in micro-fragmented corals. It alludes to the reality of a biological process phenomenon taking place to prove this is not just an illusion.[1]

Image 18.1

Micro-fragmenting a piece of coral using a diamond band saw. The micro-fragments generated will contain a few polyps each and will then be placed on ceramic plugs.

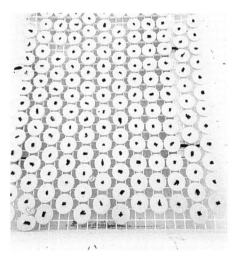

Image 18.2

Micro-fragments of elkhorn coral (Acropora palmata). The micro-fragments are about 2–3 mm in size and contain 1–3 polyps each. They're on ceramic plugs that are 1.25 inches across, plenty of room for them to grow.

19

Fusion and Con-Fusion: "Bring Out Your Dead"

I F THE game-changer of coral micro-fragmentation was not amazing enough, our next related discovery really accelerated our excitement. It came about from producing more corals than we could handle using micro-fragmentation. After we first started making hundreds of micro-fragments per hour, sometimes close to a thousand in a single day, we started to run out of tanks to hold them. Consequently, we started to place them much closer together than normal due to lack of space. Remember, corals that are genetically different do not like to touch each other. They can fight with each other and sometimes go to war (Chapter 12). Even though our micro-fragmented corals were basically clones (identical twins) of the parent colony, it still needed to be confirmed that they could live harmoniously next to each other.

Thankfully, our corals did not fight with each other. Not only that, they started to grow towards each other and merge back together! Unlike some siblings I know, micro-fragments from the same parent piece get along just fine, and when they finally touch a sibling (clone) they will fuse back together to become one coral again—just larger (see Image 19.1).

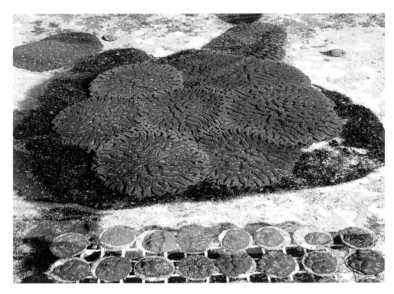

Image 19.1

A great example of fusion. At the bottom are 16 small colonies (or fragments) of knobby brain coral grown from micro-fragments. Above are 9 of these types of small colonies fused together two years later. You can clearly see the original colonies and discern their grooves merging.

Fusion and Re-Skinning

With this incredible new knowledge, we could now take one small coral the size of a golf ball, cut it into 10–100 micro-fragments, have them rapidly grow back to that golf ball size, and then plant them near each other where they will grow back together and fuse. Confused? I was too, because there is not any other animal or plant that fuses back together in this manner (that I know of). This fusion process now allows us to plant 20–100 clones from the same single parental piece onto the skeleton of a dead coral, spacing them evenly apart, all around the surface. The clones will then grow, eventually start to touch each other, and then fuse. Before too long the entire dead coral skeleton has a living coral layer on its surface. This process is called *re-skinning* and large coral head skeletons can be brought back from the grave with this new layer of life. We can essentially bring a 100–year old dead coral skeleton back to life within just a couple of years (see Images 19.2 and 19.3). Move over Lazarus, we have a lot of re-skinning to do. Bring out your dead, indeed!

Image 19.2

A completely dead skeleton of mountainous star coral with many small colonies outplanted on it. These colonies were generated from micro-fragmentation and grown on plugs. When divers outplanted them, they drilled holes into the coral skeleton and then inserted the plugs. The coral on the plugs will grow towards each other and fuse, eventually re-skinning the entire skeleton. This will bring back to life a new colony of mountainous star coral that would normally take several hundred years to grow. Photo credit: Dan Mele.

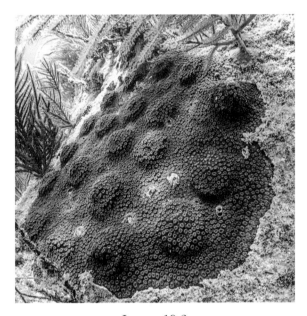

Image 19.3

Twenty small colonies of mountainous star coral have been outplanted on a coral skeleton. These small colonies are in the process of fusing together to become one large functioning colony on the reef. Photo credit: Dan Mele.

The Grateful Dead

It is astounding that we can bring a hundred or even a thousand-year-old coral skeleton back to life by placing these faster growing pieces of living tissue on its surface. To my knowledge, no other organism on earth has shown this ability to add living tissue onto the surface of a dead skeleton and have it grow. This phenomenon is so unique that I have trouble finding a good analogy in the biological world. For instance, if I told you that I could take living tissue from a Redwood or Sequoia tree and place it on the trunk of a deceased tree, and doing so would somehow bring that tree back to life, you would question my sanity. But this same process does work with corals, and this proved to be the other game-changer we needed to restore dead reefs. Working with skeletal remains of giant coral heads, we can add the spark of life again, thereby keeping the reefs functioning and growing.

Today, many reefs look like underwater graveyards of coral skeletons. Regretfully, there are no shortages of skeletons in our ocean closet, just plenty of places to start planting corals. We do not have to plant single fragments and wait decades or centuries for them to grow up into boulder size coral heads. We have lost half of the world's corals, but their skeletons are still there as monuments to their lifetime of building calcium carbonate rock-like formations. Luckily, we now have a way to bring them back into existence. Well, not *really*. We're not bringing back the dead, just borrowing their dead skeletal remains and starting from there. When diving, I now see potential surfaces to be covered by live tissue instead of just coral tombstones. Unfortunately, I have become accustomed to seeing reefs that are barely alive and have lamented the loss of the colorful beauty that was once there. Now, I focus on the few survivors, the resistant and resilient donor colonies that can be sampled and used for re-skinning projects. Regretfully, today there is no shortage of planting spots, just like there were no shortages of destroyed rainforests that now have been re-planted with billions of trees.

PART IV

The Future

20

Size Really Does Matter, Not Age!

YOU'VE PROBABLY heard the old adage "Size Matters" in a bunch of different contexts (insert your joke here). Well, when it comes to corals and reproducing—it certainly does. When corals reach a certain size, they are ready to become sexually active. The size of the coral head, not the actual age, is what tells them they are a mature coral and that they should start acting like one. Even within a newly fused or re-skinned colony, the *size* of a mature adult, although technically younger in age, will determine behavior, including sexual activity. What that means for conservation and ecological restoration is that we may not have to wait decades or centuries for outplanted corals to start sexually reproducing and adding new corals onto the reef. This is the hope for all involved with restoration efforts—that at some point the spawning population is restored so that they become self-sustaining, and we won't have to intervene with more bucket babies.

Hey Porites, What Are You Doing?

We were first made aware of this sexual phenomenon when we were working with a brooding species of *Porites* called mustard hill corals. Remember that brooding corals have both male and female colonies. The first spawning event happens when males release sperm that find their way to a female colony and then fertilize the eggs held by the female. The female broods these fertilized eggs internally until they become fully functioning larvae. These larvae are then *spawned* and usually settle nearby. *Porites* had a bad reputation among the coral elite as the "weeds" of the reef. They, as their common name sounds, range from bright green to mustard yellow—like the mustard served on hot dogs. The Atlantic species don't get as big as the more famous brain, mountain, and boulder corals. They proved, however, to be a great scientific tool as they can become reproductive fairly early compared to other corals, usually at about 12 years old, while ranging in size from somewhere between a softball and a basketball (Image 20.1).

Because *Porites* are brooders, the Smithsonian Marine Laboratory utilized them to conduct research experiments on the swimming larval stage and both its settlement cues and survival, as well as the effects on it from other compounds, chemicals, and organisms in its environment. It was a terrific model for experimentation in laboratories, as adult coral heads were temporarily moved from the wild and transported to the laboratory during the weeks that they usually reproduce—during the new moon (not full moon) and in the spring months of the year. Using modified water pitchers, each coral head was placed in a single pitcher and supplied with flowing water so that when any larvae were released during the night they would swim, flow out over the spout, and be collected in a fine mesh screen. Then in the morning anxious scientists and student helpers would collect and count the retained larvae and use them

Image 20.1
Mustard hill coral on a patch reef in the Bahamas.
Photo credit: James St. John, CC BY 2.0,
https://creativecommons.org/licenses/by/2.0 via Wikimedia Commons.

in their designed experiments conducted over the next few days. This was done on a regular basis at the Mote Tropical Research Lab by the Smithsonian group during this same spring event each year.

On one occasion I inquired how old these scientists thought the grapefruit-sized reproductive colonies were and they gave me an age range of 12 to 20 years. I remarked that we had just finished a fusion experiment and had some colonies of *Porites* that were the same size in our tanks. Like all inquisitive scientists we immediately set up a few more of these modified water pitcher culture vessels and placed our few fused colonies in each of them. We also waited overnight and anxiously scrambled to see the results first thing in the morning. And lo and behold, there were live swimming larvae that had been released from these few fused colonies as well (apparently, we had male and female fused colonies in the same tanks!). When, during this excitement, they asked me how old these colonies were, I exclaimed, "only 11 months old!"

Our curiosity piqued, we continued to follow these collected swimming larvae to see if they were even competent to settle and grow into primary polyps. They looked healthy—in fact they appeared larger and darker than those collected from the older wild coral heads. But maybe they were just "shooting blanks" and these larvae were not going to develop. However, that was not the case. They turned out to be viable larvae that settled and developed just as well as the natural wild colonies.

This observation was quite remarkable and proved the point from which we began this chapter—within this coral species, *size mattered, not age*, when it came to sexual reproduction. It also opened us up to the bigger, more important question: could we speed up the growth of other coral species through fusion, enabling them to reach the size of adult colonies much faster and thereby able to reproduce earlier in their life cycle? Fortunately, the answer to that question is *yes*! From 2013–2018, my staff from Mote and I outplanted multiple colonies of mountainous star coral (*Orbicella faveolata*), a broadcast spawner. We arranged them in groups of 5, 10, and 20 fragments, in areas the diameter of softballs, basketballs, and large pizza pies respectively. They fused back together into colony sizes resembling 25–75-year-old corals. Then in 2020, Mote postdoctoral fellow Dr. Hanna Koch biopsied them in early summer and found them to be developing gametes. In August 2020, she witnessed the first spawning of these same massive corals that we had outplanted a few years earlier (Images 20.2–20.3). Over 85% of these corals had spawned. Getting corals to reproductive size quickly through fusion is yet another game-changer for corals, essentially an extension of the marvels of micro-fragmentation.

Fusion is an amazing technique used for coral restoration. It enables scientists to select corals with favorable traits and then grow them to sexual maturity much faster. Scientists can then conduct genetic crossings every few years without having to

Image 20.2

From 2013 to 2018, we outplanted various sized arrays of micro-fragmented mountainous star corals off Cook Island in the Florida Keys. This array of newly outplanted micro-fragments was about the size of a large pizza.

Image 20.3

Within 2–5 years, these arrays, outplanted by the author, fused into colonies, many becoming sexually mature and spawning like the one shown here with Hanna Koch. Photo credit: Hanna Koch.

wait decades for nature to do it. This can allow for relatively quick results, similar to those that occurred when organisms that reproduced quickly were used for genetic research, like fruit flies and peas. When scientists used fast growing plants to select attributes desired for use in agriculture, they were quickly able to grow and cross pollinate them. Crossing green smooth peas with yellow wrinkly ones and so forth could be done every year. Remarkably, we are now at the point where we can do this every few years for corals. In the span of time a graduate student is at school, they could potentially cross corals that grow up to be crossable again. This is an extraordinary way to assist Mother Nature in restoring coral reefs— by having sexually active corals available within a few years instead of waiting for decades.

Selective Rapid Growth Cycle

My Eureka Mistake, along with the additional discoveries of fusion and early reproduction from re-skinned coral skeletons, can now be put into a sequenced order called the *Selective Rapid Growth Cycle* (SRGC)—also known as the Vaughan Cycle. This cycle uses the process *frag-fuse-mature-spawn-cross-settle* to quickly advance coral genetics through selective breeding.[1] Consequently, if there is a species of corals in which some strains are found to be thriving under some conditions, while other strains of the same species do well under other conditions, the SRGC can be used to maximize the qualities of both in future coral generations. The best of both worlds!

For example, if one genetic strain of coral was resistant to a particular disease but susceptible to coral bleaching, and another genetic strain of the same species was not resistant to the same disease but was more resistant to coral bleaching, both strains may not do well under summer bleaching conditions when the disease is also present. To take advantage of their genetic qualities, you can take a small amount of tissue from each, cut them into many micro-fragments, and then grow fragments of each separately in a large arrangement so they can fuse. Each newly fused colony should reach reproductive size in just a few years. Once they spawn, the gametes from each can be captured and fertilized in a lab, hopefully producing hundreds of surviving larvae. Certain members of this next generation should receive the genes for both resistance to the disease and resistance to bleaching from both parents. Of course, there will be some who wind up with the worst traits of both parents. These kinds of selective breeding activities have been done for years with agricultural plants, farm animals, racehorses, and dog breeds. We can now do this with corals in the time span that we have been able to do it with other species. We should be able to use SRGC (not gene-jockeying or splicing) to select and watch for the attributes of corals that can survive the current stresses from climate change and various emerging diseases.

Using fusion to grow corals to a sexually mature size quickly is a great tool for future coral restoration culturists that want to grow corals in nurseries for restoration. This "assisted evolution" was the focus of the late coral scientist, Dr. Ruth Gates. On the other side of the globe, she was pursuing "Super Coral" from branching corals in Kaneohe Bay in Hawaii, focusing on genetic strains that had survived bleaching events. She would cross them in the labs at the Coconut Island Marine Lab as part of programs at the University of Hawaii, funded by the Alan Family Foundation. This was an excellent use of selective breeding of the fast-growing branching corals. We now know that we can selectively breed both the branching and massive species of coral for advantageous traits to enhance the survival of corals and their reef communities.

21

Scaling Up Coral Production

THE TERM *large scale* in coral restoration is relative to what has been done in the past. The ocean itself is large in scale, but we have only just begun to cultivate corals in the tens of thousands. A few nurseries have grown close to a hundred thousand corals, but it has taken anywhere from two to ten years to produce this number. My personal tally to date is 100,000 corals, and my new goal is 1 million before I retire. This number is significant enough to make an aquaculture production model for corals that can then expand exponentially, as has been done for clams, oysters, and shrimp. It is similar to the goal of the Nature Conservancy campaign from over a decade ago to plant one billion trees to restore forests across the globe. That number has long since been left behind with over 8 billion trees planted since program inception.[1]

So, you may wonder, "How can this scaling up process be physically implemented with underwater corals?" Could it take thousands of divers, tens of thousands of employed fishermen, private-public partnerships, and volunteers? The answer is most likely "yes" to all of those, but only if there is funding. Right now, minimal levels of public and private financial support exist. What we need is funding that represents the real value of coral reefs, including the associated billions of dollars in tourism and trillions of dollars in value for both shoreline protection and coastal storm damage control. Many are making a living wage on the water, while others rely on the living reef for subsistence food gathering. Put all of these values together and we should have started doing this resource enhancement many years ago. By speeding up coral reef restoration with technological advances, we can scale up the numbers of corals produced and lower the cost of production.

There are a few examples that show how start-up projects have enormous costs versus the number of corals produced. Many were experiments or demonstrations run by governmental agencies or research foundations trying to show that growing corals at scale can work. However, they did not reach farm culture production levels, which need to be attained in order to produce corals at scale with reasonable associated costs. Our first attempt at producing the massive species of corals in a land-based nursery, done the old-fashioned way prior to micro-fragmentation, produced only 600 corals in the first six years. Waiting for a coral to grow for 1–2 years, then cutting it in half to make two more, then waiting another few years to do it again, has little return on investment. The research from this effort was invaluable, but costly, to the tune of over $1,000 per coral.

It's a Farm, Not a Laboratory!

After my Eureka Mistake with micro-fragmentation, we were eventually producing 600 or more corals a day. This brought the cost down to under $100 per coral. By the time we were producing 10,000 corals per year with the same staff, the cost per coral came down to $25. With a production capacity of 25,000 corals per year, the price per coral drops to $10 each.

Now that's more like it! Real production farms should be able to produce and outplant corals for about $2 per coral when they are producing 50–100,000 corals each year with the same staff and facilities. They can even go faster if they are actual production farms and not agencies with scientists also doing research and conducting experimentation. Production of numbers at scale produces a good economy of scale, that is all there is to it—even when it comes to corals. Our battle-cry needs to be: *"It's a farm, not a laboratory!"*

What about other advances to get to large-scale production? If we learn from the scaling up processes for other aquatic species, we see that repetition of small culture systems may not be the answer. For example, when shrimp farmers determined they could first grow a shrimp larvae in petri dishes, they did not start ordering millions of petri dishes. Instead, they increased the size of the vessel used to culture the larvae. Other shellfish hatcheries did the same thing. Likewise, if it takes one technician an hour to drain and clean a 100-gallon larval tank with a thousand larvae, but it takes the same time to drain and clean a 10,000-gallon tank with 10 million larvae, scale is achieved through the sizing of the equipment. Or, if they improve the nutritional component of the feeds and grow the larvae bigger and faster, efficiency is improved as the larvae grow more quickly.

Almost all the advanced seafood aquaculture hatcheries specialized into hatchery, nursery, and field grow-out operations. Further specialization of broodstock development, genetic selection, feed production, maintenance providers, product harvesting, and processing specialties only evolved once the industry matured and developed. Consider land agriculture: a farmer does not make his own tractor, harvester, or specialized seeds. In aquaculture for food species, it has been the same. For some reason though, the aquaculture of corals for restoration is dominated by governmental agencies or research organizations whose approach fails to learn from these other industries.

Can you imagine if we still had scientists trying to scale up food production by developing new crop seeds while also farming the corn by hand with a shovel and hoe? Or university, agency, or non-profit foundation staff milking cows or harvesting tomatoes one at a time to keep up with the scale required to feed the world? Likewise, scientists do not have to be the ones to outplant corals, as others can be easily trained and employed to do this work. Let's promote the understanding that coral restoration can be scaled up and is no longer a slow and tedious process.

No Robots Required

So, do we need to design and build a robot to outplant corals? No, let's not put the cart before the horse as we don't yet produce enough corals to think about automation of their final placement. It takes about six months to grow a coral, but only a minute to outplant it. Let's get to scale with production first before automating the very last step. Instead, we should actually look to use the vast labor pool of local divers and fisherman who work on the water to help with these efforts. They handle boats, work in all types of weather and sea conditions, know the area, and have a vested interest in the reefs being revitalized and protected. We don't need an Xprize for automated robots to outplant corals (one was awarded years ago, but plans fell though),[2] we need efficient and effective ways to grow them at scale and at a low cost. Once there, local environmental stewards, fishermen, and divers can do the rest. This is the real hope for the future of our coral reefs.

22

New Tools of the Trade

I F WE look at tool development in any other trade (carpentry, farming, computers, etc.), we would see a progression of innovative tools that increase production efficiency while lowering the costs of their respective tasks. True, carpentry has been around for thousands of years and a hammer is still a hammer, but tools like the electric drill, circular saw, chop saw, and pneumatic nail guns have dramatically sped up the process for building houses and furniture. Land farming has had its fair share of tool development from simple tools like the shovel or hoe, to tractors and modern agricultural combines that can cover hundreds of acres. Tools for computers have advanced tremendously with the advent of higher speed processors and memory chips that can store a virtual library on something the size of a postage stamp. For aquaculture, there was not so much a progression of tools but more of a progression of techniques using already available tanks, pipes, pumps, and valves—all essentially borrowed from existing water treatment systems, swimming pool supplies, and home aquarium equipment.

From Concrete Blocks to Shipping Containers

In coral reef restoration, concrete blocks from the building industry can be used to provide bases for coral field nurseries. Advancements from there have included variations of the cement base, the plug or puck the coral was attached to, and improvements for easy handling and attachment to nursery areas. Monofilament strands employed by fishermen are used to suspend nursery lines, or nets, keeping the substrates that hold corals aligned vertically and off the bottom of the ocean floor. Metal rebar used to reinforce cement in construction on land is bent to form table-like structures that corals can be attached to during the nursery phase. These methods are not too different than previous methods to grow oysters, clams, sponges, or seaweed anywhere around the world in the last century.

One newer tool that has recently evolved is the *coral tree*, a more 3-dimensional culture tool that supports branching corals and keeps them off the bottom of the ocean (discussed in Chapter 17). Micro-fragmentation and fusion represent great advancements, but again, these are techniques or methods still awaiting the next evolutionary step forward in the tools employed to ultimately speed up the process and potentially reduce the resources required. Perhaps coral culture for restoration will be able to utilize some of the tools designed for underwater exploration.[1] Let's look at some of those tool advancements that could be included with the coral restoration process.

As discussed in Chapter 13, there are some similarities between space and the deep sea, primarily because neither place is our natural environment and exploration requires extensive equipment. The space industry has had many sponsored developments, inventions, and improvements based on National Aeronautics and Space Administration (NASA) funding and now private funding from billionaires. The National Oceanic and Atmospheric Administration (NOAA) and private industry have both borrowed many ideas and concepts from the space industry, however, with much less available funding. Examples include Remotely Operated Vehicles (ROVs), Autonomous Underwater Vehicles (AUVs), and underwater drones. All three are finding their way from the oceanographic realm and offshore petroleum industries to commercial aquaculture and now ocean conservation. This type of automation is already being used to monitor coral growth, survival, and environmental parameters. Multiple photographs and videos are now taken across larger areas and stitched together like a quilt, using computer graphics to provide a reef size view called a *photo mosaic*. This view can then be analyzed using *photogrammetry*, which is a technique to obtain reliable data and measurements of real-world objects in the environment by creating 3D models from photos. Also, multi-wavelength cameras can see what we cannot and tell us more about coral health and stressors.[2]

One simple engineering feat that has recently been developed is a *Coral Restoration Unit* (CRU). This is essentially a self-contained land-based coral nursery system in a box. The beauty of it is that it can be transported anywhere in the world. My Plant a Million Corals Foundation pioneered the design and development of this aquaculture nursery system. It is built inside of a shipping container and provides an all-in-one coral nursery production unit. Systems within this unit are complete with pumps, pipes, valves, filters, and tanks, and now even solar powered versions can be set up in locations with no electricity. Plant a Million Corals is creating opportunities for sponsors and other foundations to financially support these units in island countries of their choosing. It is important to distribute CRUs to those who can't afford to engineer their own coral restoration systems—or even get the pieces, parts, and equipment to do so. A turn-key coral production unit that people around the world can use to grow on their own will substantially increase the global number of corals (Images 22.1–22.3).

Image 22.1

A 40-foot-long insulated shipping container custom built into a transportable coral land nursery features six (3 feet × 8 feet × 1 foot) rectangular fiberglass tanks (on the right) and two white storage tanks (on the left). Once the container arrives, these fiberglass tanks are removed and connected to plumbing. This is where the coral fragments will grow. The two white storage tanks become part of the water treatment and filtration system.

Image 22.2

The water filtration system is assembled in the shipping container once the six fiberglass tanks are set up outside.

Image 22.3

The side of the container opens up easily so all parts can quickly go back inside and be secured during a storm. These CPUs are destined for Puerto Rico and South Pacific Islands.

Plant a Million Corals

The idea of planting a million corals developed during a few informal meetings with colleagues who were working on staghorn coral restoration projects. Friends from Florida Fish and Wildlife, The Nature Conservancy, Mote Marine Lab, and the Coral Restoration Foundation shared ideas for how we could come up with the necessary funding for continued coral reef restoration.

First, we had to determine how many corals we wanted to produce, and this had to be an obtainable goal. The Nature Conservancy had launched a similar project called "Plant a Billion Trees" in the world's rainforests so we knew we needed a big (but realistic) number. So we started doing the math, and chose a target of 1,000,000 corals in 10 years. At a cost of $100 per coral, this would mean a fundraising goal of $100 million. My gut feeling was that $100 per coral was too high and $100 million too unrealistic. We needed to grow corals quickly and at scale for a much lower cost, so I started focusing my time and energy in that direction instead.

Around that same time, I attended a Renaissance Conference (no, we didn't dress up like medieval characters), where renaissance-type thinkers gather to share ideas on "how to create a better world." After being introduced as the guy who grows corals and restores reefs, I mentioned that "If I had $10 million, I could take the elkhorn coral off the endangered species list in just ten years." At the end of my talk, some attendees started asking me for the name of my non-profit so they could try and raise those funds before the end of the conference. But there was one big problem, I did not have my non-profit foundation ready yet. This lost opportunity spurred me into action and some months later, with the guidance and help of friends and colleagues, I was able to officially launch a 501(c)(3) non-profit foundation called Plant a Million Corals, complete with an amazing amount of energy and determination to reach our goal.

Today our headquarters is a coral farm on Summerland Key in the Florida Keys. Our current goal is not just to produce one million corals overall, but one million corals *each year*. We will then coordinate the outplanting of the corals through various organizations around the globe. In addition, I am working to train people in the techniques of active coral restoration at dozens of locations. As these efforts align, it gives me hope for a new and simpler goal. Someday soon it is my intention to put through the paperwork that will change the name of our foundation by swapping out a single letter, transforming it from "Plant a *Million* Corals" to "Plant a *Billion* Corals."

23

Speed Bumps

IN RECENT years I have had the honor of giving lectures on coral restoration to the Boy Scouts of America at Florida Sea Base Camps. Often, I start off my talks like a magic show by pretending to be a mind reader. I tell the audience that my talk will be about how I plan to plant a million corals before I retire. Slowly closing my eyes, I pretend to read their minds and then look around the audience as if I am able to decipher their thoughts. Then I say, "Most of you are probably wondering how I can plant a million corals because they can take hundreds of years to grow? Right?" And everyone smiles and nods their heads in agreement. "Many of you are also wondering how I can do all that before I retire since I look like I am 100 years old already." They laugh until I tell them that I have already planted over 100,000 corals and that if I had more funding, I could easily complete the goal in as little as a year's time!

Once I have their undivided attention, I proceed to illustrate the benefits of micro-fragmentation by doing a simple math exercise. The exercise is this: if you had one tank of

400 elkhorn coral fragments and cut them into an average of 50 micro-fragments each, then 20,000 new coral micro-fragments would be produced. Then in as little as 6 months, when they reach a certain size, you cut each of them into 50 more micro-fragments. Now how many total coral fragments do you have? Yes, for those without calculators, it would be 1,000,000 and you could be ready to plant a million corals in less than one year from today! Easy, right?

Yes, it could be, as this is a future that is very possible today. Imagine doing this for five more years and producing two crops a year—that would mean a total of 10,000,000 corals could be produced with the same tanks and facilities. Or if you had the capacity to expand the number of tanks and systems each time, you could get to 100,000,000 in only 18 months and half a billion in just two years. It would be theoretically possible to take elkhorn coral off the Endangered Species list in Florida in just those few years. What other organism can you forecast the future for in this way? If we could do this with the polar bear, panda bear, or rhino, it would be an earth-changing event. Unfortunately, micro-fragmentation only works for corals, but if we were not restricted by funding, space, labor, or permits, we could do this with almost every coral species. This is a future we can forecast. This is a future we can accomplish.

Alright, it sounds like an easy solution so what could go wrong? Well, there are a few speed bumps that need to be addressed. Micro-fragmentation allows us to grow corals much faster than we ever thought possible. Relatively speaking, the acceptance of this technique by the established scientific community, regulatory agencies, and funding entities has been much slower. Part of this is due to the fact that long-term monitoring of outplanted corals that originated from micro-fragments needs to take place to ensure the corals are doing well—and this takes time. Next, we will briefly explore this factor and other speed bumps on the freeway to the future.

Long-Term Monitoring—How Are the Outplanted Corals Doing?

Long-term monitoring in active coral restoration means periodically going out to where corals are outplanted onto the reef and recording how well they are growing. Active coral restoration project sites in Indonesia (Mars Inc.) and Belize (Fragments of Hope Foundation) have shown outstanding progress in terms of coral growth and reef restoration in as little as 5–10 years. It is critical to be able to prove this success by using before and after pictures as evidence (Images 23.1–23.5). This is a winning solution: photo documentation of reefs restored back to functional coral patch reefs or larger reefs is a "seeing is believing" strategy that works. I don't know anyone who has physically witnessed the dramatic changes resulting from active coral restoration who is not immediately a full-fledged believer.

Photo documentation technologies for long-term monitoring include highly advanced photography and video techniques, including photo mosaics, photogrammetry, and autonomous underwater vehicle and underwater drone videos. These can be used over very large expanses of the reef, allowing for a comprehensive record of changes that have taken place over a period of time. Long-term monitoring is essential to documenting how well our coral restoration efforts are proceeding.

Old School, New School

There are skeptics in the scientific community since microfragmentation is a new technology, having only been developed since the 2010s, and its successes have had limited time to be processed and published in scientific literature. Many new technologies take decades to perfect and years to gain acceptance in peer-reviewed publications. And, in fact, many established reviewers in this field are those who

Mars Inc. Restoration in Indonesia

*Photos courtesy of Mars Inc. (top and middle)
and the Ocean Agency (bottom)*

Image 23.1
*A dead, rubble
covered site
in Bontosua,
Indonesia.*

Image 23.2
*Reef stars (inset)
that Mars
developed with coral
fragments attached
to them, which were
then interconnected
and secured to the
sea bed.*

Image 23.3
*The same site
36 months later
showing the reef
stars have been
fully integrated
into a functioning
reef.*

Fragments of Hope Restoration in Belize

*(Photos courtesy of Lisa Carnes, Executive
Director and Founder of Fragments of Hope)*

Image 23.4

*This photo from October 2011 shows degraded reef rubble with an
outplant of elkhorn coral (Acropora palmata) at a site in Laughing
Bird Caye National Park, Belize.*

Image 23.5

*The same site in May 2016 showing a successfully restored and
functioning reef teeming with fish and invertebrates.*

originally published the standard natural growth rates of corals in nature (which are slow), and are unfamiliar with this new technology. Those who are familiar seem to have a hard time believing the faster coral growth rates resulting from micro-fragmentation and the statistics it generates. Furthermore, it can be very difficult to have new, outside-the-box discoveries published in "old school" journals.

Luckily, journals are not the only way to communicate scientific information anymore. Newer media platforms have catapulted this game-changing information to reach millions. The first American Association of Retired Persons (AARP) video that I did[1] highlighted my Eureka Mistake and I was later honored to be nominated as one of the 25 people they call "myth busters." Myth busters, according to the AARP, are people who do not let age get in their way of moving forward with their goals.[2] In fact, my quote, "I am not going to retire until I plant a million corals" was caught on this AARP video and is now immortalized as the name of my foundation: Plant A Million Corals. Essentially, "plant a million corals" is both our vision and our mission statement—sweet and simple.

The AARP video received over 20 million views and plenty of shares (even by Jimmy Buffet). I also have had a lot of opportunity to share my vision through Ted Talks which have also gone viral resulting in wonderful support from various celebrities. Social media can spread information so much faster, and in a race against time and extinction, faster is what we need.

Permitting for Restoration

Another speed bump to restoration comes in the form of regulatory roadblocks. This has occurred within the permitting processes, particularly within the U.S. For example, in the Florida Keys, once corals have been produced via micro-fragmentation, a permit is required by the National Oceanic and Atmospheric Association (NOAA) and the Florida Fish and Wildlife Conservation Commission (FWC) to outplant corals back onto the reef.

The intention is good, in that you do not want sick or non-native corals being planted onto local reefs, and there should be a certain amount of follow-up monitoring. However, this permitting process can take a very long time. It took six full years to get my first permit to outplant corals! It is not ideal to have corals that are ready to be outplanted onto a reef sitting in tanks on land for years and years while waiting for a permit. The corals can survive in the tanks, but this creates an unnecessary bottleneck in restoration, as there is now no more room in the tanks to grow out new micro-fragments. Hopefully, as we move forward, the permitting process will become more streamlined with less duplication of effort. I have worked all over the world assisting different countries with coral reef restoration and every country is different in their permitting requirements.

Money

There is no standard financial support for the funding of active coral reef restoration at present. Restoration on land is typically well-funded by governmental agencies via tax dollars, and occasionally parties that may have disturbed a wetland or natural area are forced to take responsibility. They usually have the option, mandated by a regulatory agency, to either do the restoration work themselves or contract it out. If they do not comply, they must pay a fine that will be used to pay for the work to be done by another party.

Underwater coral reef restoration was first prompted only by the damage caused by boats and ships moving across areas populated by coral reefs where the ships would break apart coral colonies when stuck or grounded. The party responsible for the damaged reef would then have to pay penalties. However, the early restoration methods for vessel groundings, developed over 15 years ago, were only geared toward sub-surface stabilization of the disturbed reef rock and rubble to prevent further erosion—not active restoration with living corals.[3]

More recently, active coral restoration technologies have become the preferred remedy for even the last holdouts of those resource managers who had thought that Mother Nature, if left alone, would come back to her previous glorious complexity.[4] This has led to a whole diversity of new technological methods and procedures being utilized around the world. You can find discussion of these case studies in *Active Coral Restoration: Techniques for a Changing Planet*. This book, with contributed chapters and case studies from the foremost coral scientists from around the world—in addition to social media amplification—has led to a more favorable working environment for obtaining financial support for reef restoration than ever before.

There has always been financial support for commercial operations of aquatic production of other marine organisms, but only for either food consumption or the aquarium trade. Historically, entrepreneurs and investors haven't come running to put their money down and provide financial backing for the production and placement of coral back into the ocean—despite the promise of an outcome that will serve the betterment of humanity. Fortunately, some foundations and philanthropic donors have started to step up to the table because governments have been slow to jump in.

Industries centered around scuba diving have been reluctant to respond as well. Their concern was that doing so would send a signal that the reefs are in trouble and that your dive trip may be disappointing as a result. The reefs, however, are in trouble, and the divers know it better than most. Divers typically discuss their trips, relaying which reef or island location they visited and which ones they enjoyed the most. Their enjoyment was not necessarily based on one location being better than the other, but the time period in which they made their dives. Reefs all over the world are in decline relative to their previous glory. Favorite dive spots from the 1960s, 70s, and 80s were spectacular compared to how they look today due to coral decline and the resulting loss of fish and other creatures that populated once healthy reefs.

Dollars and Cents

So, what are the financial considerations of active coral restoration in terms of real costs—"dollars and cents" or "logic and sense?" First, the financial component is the dollar value of reefs and the cost in money to restore them. The values attributed to coral reefs are reflected in their ecological function and are calculated by their contributions to fisheries, commerce, tourism, and, more recently, shoreline protection. These values were usually derived from economists who were charged with evaluating the damage from vessel groundings to produce a number for documenting and substantiating fines levied for these kinds of disturbances.

    These numbers were also used to justify the preservation of *marine protected areas* with an economic impact analysis to justify the protection. The initial valuations were usually underestimated but are now more realistic as new factors are incorporated into the equation. Among them are the biological, social, and geological services which, until a few years ago, were not well understood or studied. Even today our biological understanding of coral reef ecosystems falls far short of all terrestrial and many aquatic systems in terms of nutrient production and cycling, as well as the complexity of food webs.

    This makes it very difficult to assign values when data and full understanding are limited and diverse. It is estimated that 25–40% of the world's fisheries are dependent on a functioning reef system, so the numbers can be huge.[5] However, that range represents a large spread to be multiplying a fishery value to, especially if based on seafood landings, sales, or ecological function. In addition, the assorted shapes and sizes of reef structures present a complex challenge in how they are appraised and factored. Is a dense but long and thin barrier reef calculated by square meters or linear miles? Are shallow patch reefs with more space between corals than the patch itself based on the area of the patch or the entire region? Do the organisms that inhabit a reef have to be full-time residents or does seasonal utilization count as a dependency? If the reef is a breeding ground for only a week or two out of its entire life cycle, how then is its importance calculated? What used to be called a food chain, a simple line drawn between different levels of organisms from producers to consumers and decomposers, is no longer an acceptable diagram. Food webs, with multiple lines and circles and connections, are the norm for a complex ecosystem such as a coral reef. Understanding one of these diagrams that looks more like a spider web with feedback loops can be harder to fully comprehend.

The bottom line is that coral reefs have only recently seen an uptick in value at a rate proportional to how fast we are losing them. By one estimate, coral reefs provide economic goods and services worth about $375 billion each year. NOAA suggests that coral reefs in southeast Florida have an asset value of $8.5 billion, generating $4.4 billion in local sales, $2 billion in local income, and 70,400 full- and part-time jobs.[6] Back in 2009, *ScienceDaily* reported the value per hectare per year of coral reefs ranged from $130,000 to $1,200,000.[7] More recent estimates, which include natural resource services, valuate coral reefs as nearing a trillion dollars—that's 12 zeroes![8]

Logic and Sense

Obviously, we really don't know the real value of an ecosystem if we don't completely understand its processes. Like the line from the great song *Big Yellow Taxi* by Joni Mitchell, "You don't know what you've got, till it's gone." We may never know the real ecological values of coral reefs until we see the compilation of all lost revenues. So, we have to use some simple logic to make sense of how important coral reefs are. We hear of tipping points, lynchpins, and the cascades to collapse—and wonder how it could ever get this far along without us knowing better.

For modern people, it is a slow rise in average temperature over our last 30–50 years, but to coral reefs that are mostly 7,000–10,000 years old, it is barely an instant. For the pH scale to drop to 7.9, and at times even lower, in locations such as our inshore reefs from where it was closer to 8.3 is crazy—especially when you are looking at an exponential scale. We cannot expect corals to evolve and adapt to the rapid rate of environmental change we are causing. To imagine a coral adapting to warming and more acidic water conditions in a few decades is not logical, as they have lived for many thousands of years in relatively stable conditions. Saving our fisheries, our shoreline protection, our tourism, and the oxygen we breathe from the ocean make sense, no matter the cents it takes to do it.

24

Moving Forward with Faith, Hope, and Love

We have just scratched the surface in our understanding of the "Secret Life of Corals," and with continued research and restoration we will learn even more. My hope is that the secrets revealed in this book will generate new public awareness, awe, and wonder for corals and the undersea world. Corals truly are audacious planet-ocean creatures, in that they are colonial animals (polyps) that live inside their calcium carbonate exoskeletons with their mutually symbiotic partners (zooxanthellae and microbes). They grow and make coral reefs around the world, and some coral reefs are large enough to be seen from outer space.

Their spectacular life cycle beginning with the synchronized release of gametes, the journey of the larvae through the "gauntlet of death" in ocean currents, and then back again to their benthic existence was only recently discovered. We now appreciate that not only does the growth rate and age of these living rocks span centuries, but that their skeletal rock remains for thousands of years and can benefit our lives in many ways. This, and our newer understanding of the ecological processes that coral reefs provide to our fisheries, livelihoods, and tourism, should propel us to say a heartfelt "thank you, corals" and to help ensure their survival.

Faith

My faith, work, and experiences over the course of my life has only increased my belief that we have been given this beautiful planet by a benevolent creator who has also provided us the free will to choose what we do with it. Whether or not you believe in a higher power—a creator of this marvelous universe—is your freedom of choice. Regardless of your personal thoughts on our origins, you should believe in conserving and restoring the natural resources of this place we call home. None of us should ignore the increasing environmental impacts that are growing exponentially. After all, there is no "Planet B" equipped with the type of environment we need to survive. Consequently, we should do what we can now to restore this one. What has been provided must be maintained and restored if we wish to continue to enjoy our status as living creatures, and the first step towards restoring the planet is to develop a reverence for life—all life, not just your fellow man, but everyone and everything, no matter where in the world they reside.

When Astronaut Nicole Stott wrote her book *Back to Earth*, she noted that everyone who visited the International Space Station came away with a unique reverence for all life on this planet and a new recognition of how fragile it is. When looking at earth from space you see no border lines drawn on this earthly globe and no names for artificial parcels of land. We are all Earthlings. What you do see is how fragile our planet is, complete with a small thin sliver of an atmosphere allowing us to breathe and survive.[1] What is not seen is the clear colorless carbon dioxide that is becoming a dire threat. That's not to say that all threats are invisible from space, as you can actually see the storms, fires, drought, and dust storms that are increasingly rendering portions of our home inhospitable. People are being driven from lands that no longer support life in Africa, and also from islands as in the Maldives due to sea level rise. Excessive fires and more frequent powerful storms seem to be ubiquitous. The fires that burn across large areas of land displace residents and also destroy a tremendous amount of wildlife and their habitat.

Reflecting on the Big Picture

This reverence for life can be accentuated when you "stop and smell the roses." To see an insect or a coral polyp in its own micro-universe, or the migration of birds or fish across the globe, should give you a reverence for ALL life as we know it. If we don't understand or appreciate nature, how will we be moved to save it (and ourselves in the process)? To be specific, every day is a new day, and we typically spend the majority of ours outside of the present and looking forward to the weekend or a needed vacation. So, like many philosophies and religions suggest, set aside a moment to reflect. Pause the movie we call our life—daily if possible— and enjoy the natural world that surrounds you.

As you take a moment to reflect, ponder the big picture of time and the evolution of life that has already taken place to get us here. There have been five mass extinction events in the history of the world, and yet humans have only been in existence a short while, relatively speaking. We need to make changes in how we live in terms of climate change, population control, and the conservation and restoration of natural resources, as the threat of another mass extinction is very real. The corals are proof of that. It is amazing that we are somehow conditioned to look at extinction as something that happens to other organisms and not ourselves.

Love and Hope

Jacques Cousteau once said, "For most of history, man has had to fight nature to survive; in this century he is beginning to realize that, in order to survive, he must protect it." He also famously stated, "People protect what they love." I have written this book to give readers an insight into the secret life of corals and to help them fall in love with this unique life form. I also wrote it to sound the alarm that coral reefs are now a mere shadow of what they once were, an environmental downfall that has taken place over the short period of my lifetime. When I see divers or snorkelers witness a coral reef for the very first time and come up to the surface amazed, I get a tear in my eye because they probably have no idea what the reef looked like just 20–30 years ago.

There certainly is hope, however. We can all change this path, but we must act fast—and by fast, I mean in the next ten years. For a start, we can restore our reefs by using the tools and techniques described in this book that came about through serendipitous discoveries, like my Eureka Mistake, that led to micro-fragmentation, fusion, and the re-skinning of dead coral colonies on the reef. Simultaneously, we need to stop, or at least diminish, major environmental stressors so that the Earth can heal herself. Furthermore, we must wake up from our collective illusion that we are independent from this planet and its climate, and stop with the unrestrained consumption of natural resources.

Let's All Be Better Stewards of the Planet

What habits can we change right now to become better stewards of the planet? Small simple changes in our daily lives can have a big impact for positive change. In the following pages are suggestions that I incorporate into my own life. If we all make a commitment to incorporate these practices into our daily routines, we will certainly move forward in the right direction.

The Mindful Breath

We as animals need to breathe, so every morning take a long deep breath when you first wake up. While inhaling, think about the marvel of plants, including algae, and how through photosynthesis they provide the oxygen we need. When you exhale, slowly breathe out and ponder the fact that the CO_2 you are now releasing is essential for those same plants. And while we have these wonderful exchanges of oxygen and CO_2 with plants, CO_2 is currently way out of balance in our atmosphere. This excess CO_2 is changing our climate, warming the planet, raising sea levels, and making the oceans more acidic. This can cause corals to bleach. It can also hinder corals, as well as other marine organisms, from making their calcium carbonate skeletons—which will ultimately lead to their demise.

Water and Wastewater Conundrum

Typically, everyone's morning ritual begins with a trip to the bathroom. Here is another opportunity to think about helping the planet by considering that toilets manufactured before 1982 use five to seven gallons of perfectly good water per flush.[2] And where does that go? Out of sight and out of mind for most of us. If wastewater treatment is done right, clean water is eventually returned to the environment. If not done well, it will contaminate our rivers, lakes, streams, and eventually our oceans.

In most parts of the world fresh drinking water is used to flush toilets, and we need to realize that there is a limited amount of fresh drinking water on Earth that is accessible for all to use. People need about a gallon of water to hydrate per day, more for some, less for others.[3] But we use so much more than that in our daily lives. One solution to this water/wastewater conundrum is to buy and use low flow (also called low flush) toilets that flush a fraction of the water but remove the waste just as efficiently. Composting toilets are a good choice to install too, especially in environmentally sensitive areas such as vacation homes, cabins, etc.

Also be conscious of the water you do use. Simple changes can go a long way to conserving water. For example, don't keep the water running while you brush your teeth or shampoo your hair. In the kitchen turn the water off while you scrub the dishes, pots, and pans. For your lawn and garden, consider plants and grasses that don't require as much water, perhaps even try xeriscape.

Reducing our Carbon Footprint

How we move around in our environment, and the activities we take part in, can have a large impact on our environment. We can go anywhere in the world relatively quickly, but at what cost? Transportation efforts emit a huge amount of CO_2 into our atmosphere. Airplanes, cars, trucks, buses, ships, recreational boats, etc., have all gotten more efficient over the last few decades but still burn fossil fuels at an alarming rate. Hopefully, sustainable vehicles will continue to gain in popularity. More and more hybrid and electric cars and trucks are hitting the market daily. Off road, I have converted my sailboat to total solar electric drives. I often ride my bike to the store, and yes, even walk—or in my case paddle—to work. I do this for the corals, the fish, and our future. You may not all be able to canoe to work, but you may be able to carpool, take public transportation, etc. All of this adds up—or should I say subtracts down—the fossil fuel burned when we travel.

Eat Down the Food Chain

The way food is produced and consumed is another big contributor to climate change. In short, the amount of grassland and forest that is turned into grazing land for cattle is increasing in order to keep up with the ever-growing human population's demand for meat and dairy. But do we really need to eat so much meat? We can certainly eat farther down the food chain then we have been doing recently. The adage that it takes ten times more land, water, and energy to grow cattle and other animals than to directly eat what plants provide is starting to take hold, not only for the sake of the environment but for health benefits, too. Dried fruits, nuts, beans, and vegetables are great staples for your pantry. You can even make some of them yourself with solar dryers! Eating down the terrestrial food chain can be a healthier and less expensive way to feed yourself. Even replacing meat once a week can make a big difference.

For the ocean, I encourage the same mantra—eat down the food chain—but leave the krill for the whales and get your omega 3s from plant sources. If you eat fish, make sure it is a sustainable species. The field of aquaculture has struggled to produce a profitable technology that is sustainable, but this is changing rapidly. The days of old ocean net pen methods, pond cultures, and chemicals that are not healthy and non-sustainable are gone. Over half the world's seafood is now farmed and the market and regulations have driven the operations to be cleaner and more responsible. Wild catch will someday be only "catch and release" or only regulated as sustainable, safe, and healthy. Do your part as a consumer to change the way things are grown, what is grown, and how it affects your health and our ecosystems.

Recycle

Recycling became mainstream long ago, but this might have us believing that anything can be recycled and it's ok to consume as much as we want because we recycle what we can. In reality, there are many myths about recycling that deserve your attention.[4] Increasingly, everything we now buy is packaged, canned, boxed, sealed, or wrapped in more ways than the product may be worth. Check out the amount of material that is in the packaging of your next delivery. This intention for preserving and protecting the product makes new waste that needs to be reduced, reused, or recycled. We have moved far past the point of just recycling a few aluminum cans and thinking we have then saved the earth. Of course, every bit helps and if we all do our part it makes a difference. Think if we just order/consume one less product per week.

Moving Forward

We need to acknowledge that we each play a role in being stewards of the Earth, no matter how small or how large, and that is what will make all the difference. The size of our personal and collective carbon footprint and our impact on natural resources is something that can be changed. We all need housing, food, water, and the ability to live comfortably, while also enjoying some free time. We all eat and consume plants and animals. We all excrete our wastes, and there are now almost eight billion of us on this planet doing that and more on a daily basis.

With this in mind, please understand that it is always better to save something from demise than to try and bring it back after it's gone. There are a lot more things that need fixing than ever before, especially our coral reefs. If we don't fix our planet quickly, and with more global effort, the planet will inevitably fix itself by moving us out of the picture. Corals will come back again as they did before, but we might not be here to see it. To avoid this end, we will need to possess a reverence and respect for life and commit to making changes for the better. Humans must awaken from their illusion of independence from the planet and its climate and stop the unrestrained consumption of its natural resources. Let us all be better stewards of the reef, the oceans, and this planet.

You now know about the secret life of corals. Please spread the word and do your part to help save them. And by doing so, you will also help to save all life on Earth.

With faith, hope, and love, let's move forward.

Finally, here are some simple things you can do to this end:

- Take a deep, mindful breath each morning and thank all plants for the oxygen they provide, including the zooxanthellae that live inside of coral
- Experience often the sunrise, sunset, moonrise, stars, or any other reminder of our tiny place in this big universe
- Stop and smell the micro-roses—all those tiny organisms that make up this working biosphere we are part of
- Watch the weather and observe the increases in global temperatures, rainfall, severe storms, droughts, floods, and overall sea level—recognize that climate change is real and happening fast
- Be observant of the change of life happening all around us, particularly to endangered species
- Appreciate that when you hear of coral bleaching occurring in the ocean that it did not happen to all the plants, trees, and grass in your neighborhood
- Be mindful of your own carbon footprint and reduce it whenever possible
- Instead of driving, walk or bike when you can—its time well spent
- Consider purchasing a hybrid or electric car or truck as your next vehicle
- Try to use computer networking and conference calls as opposed to fossil-fuel consuming travel
- Eat farther down the food chain and consider more plant proteins as substitutes for meat

* Consider eating certified, sustainably farmed fish and aquaculture products, instead of fish products that are unsustainable
* Donate to a charity of your choice that supports wildlife and restoration efforts either above or below the water
* Recycle, reduce, and reuse waste and try composting
* Consume one less (simple but effective)
* Snorkel or dive to see the reefs, while you can

Remember: we are all temporary caretakers of our planet, and our children will follow our lead.

Acknowledgments

I have tremendous awe and gratitude for the Watchful Creator, the Great Potter who transformed a simple lump of clay like me to what I have become today. Upon reflection I realize that I must have been groomed for this moment in time. My desire to scuba dive and see the undersea world was planted in my heart at a very young age. The opportunity to collect corals with university students when I was 13 seemed like divine intervention. I did not realize it then, but my early experiences with simple micro-algae, seagrasses, marine ecosystem productivity, and the scaling up of clams, oysters, and fish would eventually lead to corals—and more important, the growing of corals at scale, in numbers large enough and fast enough to make a real difference in reef restoration. My Eureka Mistake resulted in a game-changer for corals with the technique of micro-fragmentation now being practiced around the world. In retrospect, I understand it was all destiny in progress, and I am truly humbled and grateful.

This gratitude extends to my parents, family, wife (Donna), and daughter (Dee Dee) for believing in me and humoring me when needed. I am particularly thankful for Donna and Dee Dee for always being by my side. They are true blessings, and I am so grateful for the opportunity to share my life's crazy-long journey with them.

My heartfelt thanks to all the other giants in the coral science and restoration fields on whose shoulders we now launch new technologies to save and restore corals. In my first book,

Active Coral Restoration: Techniques for a Changing Planet (2021), my colleagues contributed great information and case studies of successful coral reef restoration projects from around the world. While destined to become a "coral classic," this first book was technical in nature and geared more for the scientific community. This new book, *The Secret Life of Corals: Sex, War, and Rocks that Don't Roll*, was intended to inspire everyone from all walks of life to fall in love with corals and to make the collective changes needed now for the health of the planet.

A big thank you goes to my editor Gwen Eyeington for helping to carry out this intention by thoughtfully and enthusiastically assisting in the development of the manuscript. Her dedication and patience helped me transform my story into a piece that is so much more than just my lone voice "crying in the wilderness." I also want to thank Stephen Buda of J. Ross Publishing for his belief in the importance of this work and bringing it to fruition. Last, but certainly not least, thank you dear reader for choosing this book. It is my sincere hope that it encourages you to better understand, save, and enjoy the underwater Garden of Eden I call coral reefs.

Notes

Chapter 1

1. Coral Reef Alliance. "All About Coral Reefs, Habitat and Distribution." Retrieved from https://coral.org/en/coral-reefs-101/geography/, accessed January 25, 2022.
2. NOAA. "How Much Oxygen Comes from the Ocean?" National Ocean Service website. Retrieved from oceanservice.noaa.gov/facts/ocean-oxygen.html#:~:text=At%20least%20half%20of%20Earth's,Earth%20comes%20from%20the%20ocean, accessed January 27, 2022.
3. NOAA. "Coral Reef Ecosystems." Retrieved from https://www.noaa.gov/education/resource-collections/marine-life/coral-reef-ecosystems, accessed November 2019.
4. NOAA. "How Do Coral Reefs Benefit the Economy?" Retrieved from https://oceanservice.noaa.gov/education/tutorial_corals/coral07_importance.html, accessed February 22, 2022.
5. Environmental Defense Fund. "Corals and Climate Change." Retrieved from https://www.edf.org/sites/default/files/8767_corals-and-climate-change.pdf, accessed March 22, 2022.
6. Michael Beck, Pew Marine Fellow. Interview retrieved from https://www.youtube.com/watch?v=VPmu7Ohxg B8, accessed July 17, 2020.
7. NOAA. "The Importance of Coral Reefs." Retrieved from https://oceanservice.noaa.gov/education/tutorial_corals/coral07_importance.html, accessed January 23, 2022.

8. Edwin L. Cooper, Kyle Hirabayashi, Kevin B. Strychar, and Paul W. Sammarco. 2014. "Corals and Their Potential Applications to Integrative Medicine," *Evidence-Based Complementary and Alternative Medicine*, Vol. 2014, Article ID 184959. https://doi.org/10.1155/2014/184959. https://www.hindawi.com/journals/ecam/2014/184959/.

Chapter 3

1. Science.org. "Coral and Coral Reef, Biology of Corals." Retrieved from https://science.jrank.org/pages/1786/Coral-Coral-Reef-Biology-corals.html#ixzz7MZVMknwV, accessed October 20, 2021.
2. Paul Humann and Ned DeLoach. 2002. *Reef Coral Identification*. New World Publications.

Chapter 4

1. Scientific American. "Timeline of Photosynthesis on Earth," April 7, 2008. Retrieved from https://www.scientificamerican.com/article/timeline-of-photosynthesis-on-earth/.
2. The Seaweed Site. "Phaeophyceae: Brown Algae." Retrieved from https://www.seaweed.ie/algae/phaeophyta.php, accessed February 12, 2021.
3. Ariel Pezner. 2018. "A Bad Romance—Climate Change Creates Toxic Relationship in Coral," Scripps Institution of Oceanography, Center for Marine Biodiversity and Conservation. Benthic Ecology Blog Post. Retrieved from https://cmbc.ucsd.edu/2018/05/11/a-bad-romance-climate-change-creates-toxic-relationship-in-coral/.
4. Dana Riddle. "Lighting by Number: 'Types' of Zooxanthellae and What They Tell Us," *Advanced Aquarist Online Magazine*, January 15, 2006. Retrieved from https://reefs.com/magazine/lighting-by-number-types-of-zooxanthellae-and-what-they-tell-us/.
5. Kate Quigley, Bette Willis, and Carly Kenkel. 2019. "Transgenerational Inheritance of Shuffled Symbiont Communities in the Coral *Montipora digitata*," *Sci Rep* 9, 13328. https://doi.org/10.1038/s41598-019-50045-y.

6. Hanna R. Koch. 2021. "Assisted Evolution and Coral Reef Resilience," Chapter 9, in *Active Coral Restoration: New Technologies for a Changing Planet*. David E. Vaughan, Editor, J. Ross Publishing.

7. The Nature Conservancy, Reef Resilience Network. "Bleaching Biology." Retrieved from https:// reefresilience.org/stressors/bleaching/bleaching-biology/, accessed January 5, 2022.

8. AIMS, Australia Institute of Marine Science. "Coral Bleaching." Retrieved from https://www.aims.gov.au/ docs/research/climate-change/coral-bleaching/coral -bleaching.html, accessed January 5, 2022.

9. Graham Readfearn. "Great Barrier Reef's third mass bleaching in five years the most widespread yet," *The Guardian,* April 6, 2020. Retrieved from https://www .theguardian.com/environment/2020/apr/07/great-barrier -reefs-third-mass-bleaching-in-five-years-the-most -widespread-ever.

10. Nick Visser. "Great Barrier Reef Hit With 'Grim' Sixth Mass Bleaching Event," *The Huffington Post*, March 25, 2022. Retrieved from https://www.huffpost.com/entry/ great-barrier-reef-sixth-mass-bleaching_n_623d5193e 4b0e3a314356611.

Chapter 5

1. Alejandra Hernandez, Roisin McMahon, and Tracy Ainsworth. "What We Have in Common with Corals and Their Unexplored Microbial World," *The Conversation*, September 11, 2016. Retrieved from https://the conversation.com/what-we-have-in-common-with -corals-and-their-unexplored-microbial-world-64798.

2. Nicola Davis. "The Human Microbiome: Why Our Microbes Could Be Key to Our Health," *The Guardian*, March 26, 2018. Retrieved from https://www.theguardian .com/news/2018/mar/26/the-human-microbiome-why -our-microbes-could-be-key-to-our-health.

3. Alejandra Hernandez, Roisin McMahon, and Tracy Ainsworth. "What We Have in Common with Corals and Their Unexplored Microbial World," *The*

Conversation, September 11, 2016. Retrieved from https://theconversation.com/what-we-have-in-common-with-corals-and-their-unexplored-microbial-world-64798.

4. Ibid.

5. Ibid.

6. K.B. Ritchie. 2006. Regulation of Microbial Populations by Coral Surface Mucous and Mucous Associated Bacteria. Marine Ecology Progress Series, 322:1–14.

7. Ibid.

Chapter 6

1. American Geophysical Union. "Giant Algal Bloom Sheds Light on Formation of White Cliffs of Dover," September 15, 2016. Retrieved from https://news.agu.org/press-release/giant-algal-bloom-sheds-light-on-formation-of-white-cliffs-of-dover/.

2. The Ocean Portal Team as reviewed by Jennifer Bennett, Smithsonian. "Ocean Acidification." Retrieved from https://ocean.si.edu/ocean-life/invertebrates/ocean-acidification, accessed January 25, 2022.

3. Stephen Barker and Andy Ridgwell. 2012. "Ocean Acidification," *Nature Education Knowledge* 3(10):21. Retrieved from https://www.nature.com/scitable/knowledge/library/ocean-acidification-25822734/.

4. Woods Hole Oceanographic Institution. "Scientists Pinpoint How Ocean Acidification Weakens Coral Skeletons." Retrieved from https://www.whoi.edu/press-room/news-release/scientists-identify-how-ocean-acidification-weakens-coral-skeletons/, accessed February 12, 2022.

5. Nathaniel R. Mollica et al. 2018. "Ocean Acidification Affects Coral Growth by Reducing Skeletal Density," *PNAS*, Vol. 155, No. 8. Retrieved from https://www.pnas.org/content/115/8/1754.

Chapter 7

1. NOAA Education. "How Do Stony Corals Grow?" Retrieved from https://oceanservice.noaa.gov/education/tutorial_corals/coral03_growth.html, accessed January 18, 2022.

2. Zac H. Forsman, Baruch Rinkevich, and Cynthia L. Hunter. 2006. "Investigating Fragment Size for Culturing Reef-Building Corals (*Porites lobata* and *P. compressa*) in *Ex Situ* Nurseries," *Aquaculture*, Vol. 261, Issue 1, pp. 89–97.

3. David E. Vaughan. 2021. *Active Coral Restoration: Technologies for a Changing Planet*. J. Ross Publishing, Inc.

4. NOAA Coral Reef Conservation Program. "Coral Facts." Retrieved from https://coralreef.noaa.gov/education/, accessed January 19, 2022.

5. Paul Humann and Ned DeLoach. 2002. *Reef Coral Identification*. New World Publications.

6. NOAA Fisheries. "Pillar Coral." Retrieved from https://www.fisheries.noaa.gov/species/pillar-coral, accessed March 1, 2022.

7. NOAA Education. "How Do Stony Corals Grow?" Retrieved from https://oceanservice.noaa.gov/education/tutorial_corals/coral03_growth.html, accessed January 18, 2022.

8. NOAA Coral Reef Conservation Program. "Coral Facts." Retrieved from https://coralreef.noaa.gov/education/, accessed January 19, 2022.

9. NOAA Education. "How Do Coral Reefs Form?" Retrieved from https://oceanservice.noaa.gov/education/tutorial_corals/coral04_reefs.html#:~:text=With%20growth%20rates%20of%200.3,30%2C000%2C000%20years%20to%20fully%20form, accessed February 2, 2022.

10. Sea World. "More About Corals and Coral Reefs, Habitat and Distribution." Retrieved from https://seaworld.org/animals/all-about/coral-and-coral-reefs/habitat/, accessed February 27, 2022.

11. Positive Reef Initiative. "The 4 Types of Coral Reef Formations Found in the Ocean." Retrieved from https://www.positivereefinitiative.com/en/news/20_the-4-types-of-coral-reef-formations-found-in-the-ocean, accessed March 18, 2022.

12. Fish Key West. "Patch Reef." Retrieved from https://www.fishkeywest.com/glossary/patch-reef/, accessed March 19, 2022.

13. Nicole Stott. 2021. *Back to Earth: What Life Taught Me About Our Home Planet—and Our Mission to Protect It*. Seal Press.

14. PADI. "2021 Worldwide Statistics." Retrieved from https://www.padi.com/sites/default/files/documents/ 2021-02/2021%20PADI%20Worldwide%20Statistics .pdf, accessed March 19, 2022.

Chapter 8

1. Michigan Department of Environmental Quality, Geological Survey Division. "The Petoskey Stone: Some History, Lore and Facts About the 'Petoskey Stone.'" Retrieved from https://www.michigan.gov/documents/ deq/ogs-gimdl-GGPS_263213_7.pdf, accessed January 13, 2022.
2. John Englander. "John's Blog/Newsletter: SEA LEVEL RISE NOW." Retrieved from https://johnenglander .net/400000-year-graphic-shows-sea-level-temperature -and-co2/, accessed April 13, 2022.
3. Ibid.

Chapter 9

1. Peter Harrison. Southern Cross University, "Distin-guished Professor Peter L. Harrison." Retrieved from https://www.scu.edu.au/marine-ecology-research-centre/ people/professor-peter-l-harrison/#:~:text=Peter%20was %20a%20leading%20member,Environmental%20 Research%20for%20this%20discovery, accessed April 1, 2022.
2. Che-Hung Lina, Shunichi Takahashib, Aziz J. Mullaa, and Yoko Nozawaa. 2021. "Moonrise timing is key for synchronized spawning in coral Dipsastraea speciose," *PNAS*, Vol. 118. Retrieved from https://www.pnas.org/ doi/10.1073/pnas.2101985118#footnotes.

Chapter 10

1. Donna Lu. "Inside the Fight to Save the Great Barrier Reef from Climate Change," *New Scientist*, January 6, 2021. Retrieved from https://www.newscientist.com/article/ mg24933160-700-inside-the-fight-to-save-the-great -barrier-reef-from-climate-change/, accessed April 18, 2022.

2. Karen Neely, Cynthia L. Lewis, Keri O'Neil, Cheryl M. Woodley, Jennifer Moor, Zach Ransom, Amelia Moura, Ken Nedimyer, and David Vaughan. 2021. "Saving the Last Unicorns: Genetic Rescue of Florida's Pillar Corals," *Frontiers in Marine Science*, Vol. 8.

Chapter 11

1. Saki Harill and Hajime Kayanne. 2002. "Larval Settlement of Corals in Flowing Water Using a Racetrack Flume," *Marine Technology Society Journal*, 36(1), pp. 76–79.

2. Nina Bai. "For Coral Larvae, Green Means Stop, Red Means Go," *Scientific American*, February 2011. Retrieved from https://www.scientificamerican.com/gallery/for -coral-larvae-green-means-stop-red-means-go/, accessed July 23, 2021.

3. Ashlee Lillis, Amy Apprill, Justin Suca, Cynthia Becker, Joel Llopiz, and T. Aran Mooney. 2018. "Soundscapes Influence the Settlement of the Common Caribbean Coral Porites astreoides Irrespective of Light Conditions." *Royal Society Open Science*, Vol. 5: 12. Retrieved from https://doi.org/10.1098/rsos.181358, accessed July 23, 2021.

4. Donna Lu. "Inside the Fight to Save the Great Barrier Reef from Climate Change," *New Scientist*, January 6, 2021. Retrieved from https://www.newscientist.com/ article/mg24933160-700-inside-the-fight-to-save-the -great-barrier-reef-from-climate-change/, accessed April 18, 2022.

5. NOAA. "Oil Spills and Coral Reefs, Planning and Response Considerations." Retrieved from https:// response.restoration.noaa.gov/sites/default/files/Oil _Spill_Coral.pdf, accessed April 16, 2022.

Chapter 12

1. Oshra Yosef, Yotam Popovits, Assaf Malik, et al. 2020. "A Tentacle for Every Occasion: Comparing the Hunting Tentacles and Sweeper Tentacles, Used for Territorial Competition, in the Coral *Galaxea fascicularis*." BMC *Genomics* 21, p. 548. Retrieved from https://doi.org/ 10.1186/s12864-020-06952-w, accessed September 2021.

Chapter 13

1. Rhett Herman. "How Fast Is the Earth Moving?" *Scientific American*, October 1998. Retrieved from https://www.scientificamerican.com/article/how-fast-is-the-earth-mov/#:~:text=The%20earth%20rotates%20once%20every,roughly%201%2C000%20miles%20per%20hour, accessed February 3, 2022.

2. Nicole Stott. 2021. *Back to Earth: What Life Taught Me About our Home Planet—and Our Mission to Protect It*. Seal Press.

3. NOAA Ocean Exploration. "How Does the Temperature of Ocean Water Vary?" Retrieved from https://oceanexplorer.noaa.gov/facts/temp-vary.html, accessed March 29, 2022.

4. Paul Snelgrove. 2011. *Discoveries of the Census of Marine Life: Making Ocean Life Count*. Cambridge University Press.

5. Smithsonian Ocean. "Deep Sea Corals." Retrieved from https://ocean.si.edu/ecosystems/coral-reefs/deep-sea-corals, accessed January 25, 2022.

6. Smithsonian Ocean. "Collecting Gold from the Deep Sea." Retrieved from https://ocean.si.edu/holding-tank/technology/collecting-gold-coral-deep-sea, accessed January 25, 2022.

7. Smithsonian Ocean. "Deep Sea Corals." Retrieved from https://ocean.si.edu/ecosystems/coral-reefs/deep-sea-corals, accessed January 25, 2022.

8. J. Murray Roberts, Andrew Wheeler, Andre Freiwald, and Stephen Cairns. 2009. *Cold Water Corals: The Biology and Geology of Deep-Sea Coral Habitats*. Cambridge University Press.

9. Smithsonian Ocean. "Deep Sea Corals." Retrieved from https://ocean.si.edu/ecosystems/coral-reefs/deep-sea-corals, accessed January 25, 2022.

10. National Public Radio. "Photos Document Coral Forest Annihilation." NPR Morning Edition, December 26, 2007. Retrieved from https://www.npr.org/templates/story/story.php?storyId=17102434, accessed February 27, 2022.

Chapter 14

1. Rowan Hooper. "Suzanne Simard interview: How I Uncovered the Hidden Language of Trees." *New Scientist*, April 28, 2021. Retrieved from https://www.newscientist .com/article/mg25033320-900-suzanne-simard-interview -how-i-uncovered-the-hidden-language-of-trees/, accessed January 23, 2022.

2. Eugenia Chen, Klaus Stiefel, Terrence Sejnowski, and Theodore Bullock. 2008. "Model of Traveling Waves in a Coral Nerve Network," *Journal of Comparative Physiology A*, 194(2), pp. 195–200.

3. Aquarium Genius. "Can Coral Feel Pain? The Complete Answer." Retrieved from https://aquariumgenius.com/ can-coral-feel-pain/, accessed February 2, 2022.

4. Sea World. "More About Corals and Coral Reefs—Senses." Retrieved from https://seaworld.org/animals/all-about/ coral-and-coral-reefs/senses/, accessed January 23. 2022.

5. Peter Wohlleben. 2016. *The Hidden Life of Trees*. Greystone Books.

6. Sea World. "More About Corals and Coral Reefs—Diet and Eating Habits. Retrieved from https://seaworld.org/ animals/all-about/coral-and-coral-reefs/diet/, accessed January 11, 2022.

7. Bonnie Bassler. TED-Ed Talk. Retrieved from https:// ed.ted.com/lessons/how-bacteria-talk-bonnie-bassler, accessed April 11, 2022.

8. Rocio Pena et al. "Relationship Between Quorum Sensing and Secretion System," *Frontiers in Microbiology*, June 7, 2019. Retrieved from https://doi.org/10.3389/ fmicb.2019.01100, accessed February 2, 2022.

9. Bhim Pratap Singh et al. "Editorial: Microbial Secondary Metabolites: Recent Developments and Technological Challenges," *Frontiers in Microbiology*, April 26, 2019. Retrieved from https://www.frontiersin.org/articles/ 10.3389/fmicb.2019.00914/full, accessed April 11, 2022.

10. Christopher Plain. "Corals 'Talk' to Each Other, New Study Concludes." The Debrief, May 6, 2021. Retrieved from https://thedebrief.org/corals-talk-to-each-other -new-study-concludes/, accessed February 11, 2022.

11. Greg Seaman. "Coral Reefs Communicate with Fish for Protection." Eartheasy, November 20, 2012. Retrieved from https://learn.eartheasy.com/articles/coral-reefs -communicate-with-fish-for-protection/, accessed February 13, 2022.

Chapter 15

1. Oliver Milman. "The 'Great Dying': Rapid Warming Caused Largest Extinction Event Ever, Report Says," *The Guardian*, December 6, 2018. Retrieved from https:// www.theguardian.com/environment/2018/dec/06/ global-warming-extinction-report-the-great-dying.

2. The Editors of the Encyclopedia Britannica. "K–T Extinction." *Encyclopedia Britannica*. Retrieved from https://www.britannica.com/science/K-T-extinction, accessed August 9, 2021.

3. Gal Dishon et al. 2020. "Evolutionary Traits that Enable Scleractinian Corals to Survive Mass Extinction Events," *Sci Rep* 10, p. 3903. https://doi.org/10.1038/ s41598-020-60605-2.

4. Avery Thompson. "According to Geologists, We're Living in a New Age," *Popular Mechanics*, January 31, 2022. Retrieved from https://www.popularmechanics.com/ science/environment/a22354823/according-to-geologists -were-living-in-a-new-age/, accessed March 1, 2022.

5. National Geographic Resource Library. "Anthropocene." Retrieved from https://www.nationalgeographic.org/ encyclopedia/anthropocene, accessed February 15, 2022.

6. The Ocean Portal Team as reviewed by Jennifer Bennett, Smithsonian. "Ocean Acidification." Retrieved from https://ocean.si.edu/ocean-life/invertebrates/ocean -acidification, accessed July 27, 2022.

7. World Wildlife Fund. Retrieved from https://wwf.panda .org/discover/our_focus/biodiversity/biodiversity/, accessed October 11, 2021.

Chapter 16

1. Intergovernmental Panel on Climate Change. "Climate Change 2021: The Physical Science Basis." Retrieved

from https://www.ipcc.ch/report/sixth-assessment -report-working-group-i/, accessed September 18, 2021.

2. Gal Dishon et al. 2020. "Evolutionary Traits that Enable Scleractinian Corals to Survive Mass Extinction Events," *Sci Rep* 10, p. 3903. https://doi.org/10.1038/ s41598-020-60605-2.

3. Oliver Milman. "The 'Great Dying': Rapid Warming Caused Largest Extinction Event Ever, Report Says," *The Guardian*, December 6, 2018. Retrieved from https:// www.theguardian.com/environment/2018/dec/06/ global-warming-extinction-report-the-great-dying.

4. Elizabeth Kolbert. 2014. *The Sixth Extinction: An Unnatural History*. Henry Holt and Co.

5. Alexander H. Taylor. "The Foundation of Modern Geology." Retrieved from https://publish.illinois.edu/ foundationofmoderngeology/catastrophism/, accessed May 7, 2022.

6. Alina Bykova. "Permafrost Thaw in a Warming World: The Arctic Institute's Permafrost Series Fall-Winter 2020," The Arctic Institute. Retrieved from https:// www.thearcticinstitute.org/permafrost-thaw-warming -world-arctic-institute-permafrost-series-fall-winter -2020/, accessed November 12, 2021.

7. PBS News Hour. "In 'Don't Look Up,' Director Adam McKay Makes Allegorical Plea to Follow Climate Science." Retrieved from https://www.pbs.org/newshour/show/ in-dont-look-up-director-adam-mckay-makes -allegorical-plea-to-follow-climate-science, accessed May 5, 2022.

8. Greta Thunberg speech. Cop 26 Climate Summit. November 5, 2021. Retrieved from https://www.youtube .com/watch?v=4Skl8m31JEQ, accessed February 6, 2022.

9. Wesley Stephenson. "Do the Dead Outnumber the Living?" BBC News, February 4, 2012. Retrieved from https://www.bbc.com/news/magazine-16870579, accessed September 21, 2021.

10. Intergovernmental Panel on Climate Change. "Climate Change 2021: The Physical Science Basis." Retrieved from https://www.ipcc.ch/report/sixth-assessment -report-working-group-i/, accessed September 18, 2021.

11. Suzanne Tate. 1989. *Lucky Lookdown: A Tale of a Funny Fish*. Nags Head Art, Inc.

Chapter 17

1. Ken Nedimyer. 2021. "Live Rock Farmer to Live Coral Farmer," Chapter 4, in *Active Coral Restoration: New Technologies for a Changing Planet*. David E. Vaughan, Editor, J. Ross Publishing, Inc.
2. Shai Shafir, Jaap Van Rijn, and Baruch Rinkevich. 2006. "A Mid-Water Coral Nursery." Proceedings of the 10th International Coral Reef Symposium, pp. 1674–1679.
3. Christopher Page, Nicole D. Fogarty, and David E. Vaughan. 2021. "Sexual Reproduction and Rearing Corals for Restoration," Chapter 8, in *Active Coral Restoration: New Technologies for a Changing Planet*. David E. Vaughan, Editor, J. Ross Publishing, Inc.

Chapter 18

1. Deanna Soper et al. 2022. "Growth and Cyclin-E Expression in the Stony Coral Species *Orbicella faveolata* Post-Microfragmentation," *The Biological Bulletin*, Vol. 242, No. 1.

Chapter 20

1. David E. Vaughan. 2021. *Active Coral Restoration: Technologies for a Changing Planet*. J. Ross Publishing, Inc.

Chapter 21

1. The Nature Conservancy's Plant a Billion Trees Campaign Is a Major Forest Restoration Effort with a Goal of Planting a Billion Trees Across the Planet. Retrieved from https://www.nature.org/en-us/get-involved/how-to-help/plant-a-billion/, accessed November 12, 2021.
2. Xprize Visioneering. "Saving Coral Reefs." Retrieved from https://www.xprize.org/visioneering/saving-coral-reefs, accessed November 13, 2021.

Chapter 22

1. David E. Vaughan, Sam Teicher, Gotor Jalpern, and Joe Oliver. 2019. "Building More Resilient Coral Reefs Through New Marine Technologies, Science and Models," *Journal of Marine Technology*, Vol. 53, No. 5, pp. 21–25.
2. David E. Vaughan and Ken Nedimyer. 2021. "Emerging Technologies," Chapter 22, in *Active Coral Restoration: New Technologies for a Changing Planet*. David E. Vaughan, Editor, J. Ross Publishing, Inc.

Chapter 23

1. https://www.facebook.com/AARP/videos/10155046983618960/.
2. Meghan Bogardus Cortez et al. "25 People Who Bust the Myths," *AARP The Magazine*, June/July 2016. Retrieved from https://www.aarp.org/entertainment/style-trends/info-2016/age-disrupters-photo.html#slide18, accessed January 25, 2022.
3. William F. Precht. 2006. *Coral Restoration Handbook*. CRC Press, Taylor & Francis Group.
4. Buki Rinkevich. 2021. "The Quandary of Active and Passive Reef Restoration in a Changing World," Chapter 3, in *Active Coral Restoration: New Technologies for a Changing Planet*. David E. Vaughan, Editor, J. Ross Publishing, Inc.
5. NOAA. "Coral Reef Ecosystems." Retrieved from https://www.noaa.gov/education/resource-collections/marine-life/coral-reef-ecosystems, accessed November 11, 2021.
6. NOAA. 2013. "Economics of Florida Reef Track." P. Edwards (ed.), *Summary Report: The Economic Value of U.S. Coral Reefs*. NOAA Coral Reef Conservation Program.
7. ScienceDaily. 2009. "What Are Coral Reef Services Worth? $130,000 to $1.2 Million Per Hectare, Per Year." Retrieved from https://www.sciencedaily.com/releases/2009/10/091016093913.htm#:~:text=What%20Are%20Coral%20Reef%20Services,Hectare%2C%20Per%20Year%20%2D%2D%20ScienceDaily, accessed April 15, 2022.

8. Ben Doherty and Christopher Knaus. "Loss of Coral Reefs Caused by Rising Sea Temperatures Could Cost $1tn Globally," *The Guardian*, April 11, 2017. Retrieved from https://www.theguardian.com/environment/2017/apr/12/loss-of-coral-reefs-caused-by-rising-sea-temperatures-could-cost-1tn-globally#:~:text=The%20%241%20trillion%20figure%20for,million%20people%20across%2050%20nations.

Chapter 24

1. Nicole Stott. 2021. *Back to Earth: What Life Taught Me About our Home Planet—and Our Mission to Protect It*. Seal Press.

2. Saving Water Partnership. Retrieved from https://www.savingwater.org/indoors/toilets/how-much-water-does-your-toilet-use/, accessed May 3, 2022.

3. Mayo Clinic. "Water: How Much Should You Drink Every Day?" Retrieved from https://www.mayoclinic.org/healthy-lifestyle/nutrition-and-healthy-eating/in-depth/water/art-20044256#:~:text=About%2015.5%20cups%20(3.7%20liters,fluids%20a%20day%20for%20women, accessed May 3, 2022.

4. Brightly. "6 Common Recycling Myths It's Time to Stop Believing." Retrieved from https://brightly.eco/recycling-myths/, accessed May 2, 2022.

Index

sweeping tentacles, 116–117, 118–119
tentacles with stinging cells, 114–116
weapons of mass destruction, 120–122
diatoms, 45
DiCaprio, Leo, 156
dinoflagellates, 29
disease pathogens, 40
divers, 72
DNA, 38–39
sequencing amplification, 140
Don't Look Up, 156–157
dynamite fishing, 158

Earth, 3, 125–128
Earthrise, 126–128
East Atlantic Oculina Reef, 134
ecological values, 217–219
logic and sense, 218–219
money/financial support and, 217–218
elkhorn corals, 23–24, 171–172, 172*f*
as reef builders, 175–176
test-tube baby, 177
elkhorn polyp, 110, 111*f*
encrusting corals, 62, 64*f*
endoskeletons, 45
environmental stressors, 163, 224
epidemics, 40–42
black-band disease, 41
SCTLD (stony coral tissue loss disease), 41–42
epidermis, polyps, 22
Eureka Mistake, 178

exoskeletons, 45
mollusks, 46–47
ocean acidification (OA) and, 51–53
polyps, 47–48
extinctions, 145–152
background extinction rate, 152
environmental conditions, 152
geologic time-scale analogy, 147–148
K–Pg extinction event, 146
Permian–Triassic, 146
pre-historic times, 145–147
sea level rise, 150–152, 151*f*

faith, 222–223
feeding, larvae, 110
fertilization, 95
financial support and coral restoration, 215–219
fission, 56
Flagler, Henry, 78
fleshy, flower, and cup corals, 64, 66, 67*f*
Florida Fish and Wildlife Conservation Commission (FWC), 207, 215
Florida Keys, 7, 10*f*, 41*f*, 58*f*, 75, 78, 150, 162, 163–164, 171, 176, 195*f*, 208, 214–215
bleaching events, 35
reef tract, 69
weather service marine forecasts, 8
food chain, 218, 226–227